Unmasking Your Future

Tools for Creating Your Best Life

Unmasking
Your Future

Tools for Creating Your Best Life

Judy Lekic

BOOKS

Winchester, UK
Washington, USA

First published by O-Books, 2010
O Books is an imprint of John Hunt Publishing Ltd., The Bothy, Deershot Lodge, Park Lane, Ropley,
Hants, SO24 0BE, UK
office1@o-books.net
www.o-books.com

Distribution in:	South Africa
	Stephan Phillips (pty) Ltd
UK and Europe	Email: orders@stephanphillips.com
Orca Book Services Ltd	Tel: 27 21 4489839 Telefax: 27 21 4479879
Home trade orders	Text copyright: Judy Lekic 2009
tradeorders@orcabookservices.co.uk	
Tel: 01235 465521 Fax: 01235 465555	ISBN: 978 1 84694 306 5
Export orders	Design: Stuart Davies
exportorders@orcabookservices.co.uk	
Tel: 01235 465516 or 01235 465517	All rights reserved. Except for brief quotations
Fax: 01235 465555	in critical articles or reviews, no part of this
	book may be reproduced in any manner
USA and Canada	without prior written permission from the
NBN	publishers.
custserv@nbnbooks.com	
Tel: 1 800 462 6420 Fax: 1 800 338 4550	The rights of Judy Lekic as author have been
	asserted in accordance with the Copyright,
Australia and New Zealand	Designs and Patents Act 1988.
Brumby Books	
sales@brumbybooks.com.au	A CIP catalogue record for this book is
Tel: 61 3 9761 5535 Fax: 61 3 9761 7095	available from the British Library.
Far East (offices in Singapore, Thailand,	
Hong Kong, Taiwan)	
Pansing Distribution Pte Ltd	Printed in the UK by CPI Antony Rowe
kemal@pansing.com	Printed in the USA by Offset Paperback Mfrs,
Tel: 65 6319 9939 Fax: 65 6462 5761	Inc

We operate a distinctive and ethical publishing philosophy in all
areas of its business, from its global network of authors to
production and worldwide distribution.

CONTENTS

Preface   1

Acknowledgements   2

Disclosure   3

Introduction   4

Part One: How the Past Affects Your Future   13

Chapter 1: Gaining Clarity   14

Chapter 2: Identifying Patterns & Beliefs   19

Chapter 3: Probable Lessons   69

Chapter 4: Taking Responsibility   81

Part Two: Opening To Your Inner Powers   101

Chapter 5: Inner Guidance   102

Chapter 6: Discover and Utilize Your Intuition   113

Chapter 7: How Other People's Energy Affects You   124

Part Three: Healing Modalities   133

Chapter 8: Techniques for Making Changes   134

Chapter 9: Conclusion   170

Appendix   176

Diagrams   178

Notes   182

Preface

Part I of *Unmasking Your Future* will demonstrate how to identify aspects of your life that are blocking you from manifesting your future and reaching your full potential. Thus, you will learn to identify outdated beliefs and discover if you are running the same patterns over and over. Later, you may be able to identify probable lessons you have chosen to learn in this life. This section also shows the way in which you will want to take responsibility for changing your life.

Part II This section will teach you how to open to your intuition and God connection. You will gain an understanding of how and why you should utilize your intuition. You will discover skills and disciplines that will help to reveal ways for you to open to your full power as a spiritual being. Finally, you will gain knowledge about how other people's energy may affect you and keep you blocked.

Part III teaches modalities on how to release past patterns in order to create a positive future. Modalities herein described will assist you in healing your past wounds and detail techniques to help you move towards a place of peace and empowerment.

Acknowledgements

Unmasking Your Future is dedicated to my children, Troy, S.J. and Sonia. Without their love and support, this book would not have been written. I want to give special thanks to my oldest son, Troy, for all the insight that he provided along the way. I also want to thank my ex-husband, Michael. Through his support I was able to see the impact of my own negative and outdated beliefs.

I give special thanks to Elizabeth Bishop, Ph.D. who helped me with editing. Without her guidance, I would not have made it through the final publishing stages. She gave me encouragement for which I am very grateful.

I am grateful for the many spiritual leaders under whom I have had the privilege of studying. For example, I studied with Dr. Tad James and Dr. Doreen Virtue, among others. I also appreciate all that I have learned from the writings of celebrated authors such as Louise Hay, Wayne Dyer, Sylvia Brown, Sonia Choquette, Ester and Jerry Hicks and many more. The insight of these talented healers has contributed to my life journey.

Disclosure

This book does not dispense medical advice or prescribe the use of any techniques as a form of treatment for physical, mental, emotional or medical problems. In other words, always follow the advice of your physician. This book represents a way of helping you expand your individual consciousness.

Examples in this book do not reflect the real names of clients. Instead, such names have been changed to protect client confidentiality.

Introduction

"The farther backward you can look; the farther forward you can see."
Winston Churchill

As I walked from the garage to the back door, I heard a voice behind me say, "Open the door and go inside quietly. Who else is here?"

"Just my son, S.J." I answered in a voice barely above a whisper. I could feel a sharp cold object pressed against my throat."

"Where are your other two kids?" A man's raspy voice inquired.

"They are spending the night at their friends' houses. I could hardly breathe as I answered. The knife pressed to my throat was beginning to hurt.

I glanced around at the man who was dressed in blue jeans and a short sleeve black shirt. He rudely shoved me into the house and shut the door. S. J., my middle child, was in the family room watching television. S.J. looked up and saw the man with the knife at my throat.

The man looked at S.J. and told him, "Stay right where you are. If you move, I will kill your mom."

S.J. never said a word. S.J. never moved. Fourteen years old, my son was savvy enough to do exactly what the man ordered.

On a couple of previous occasions, I had noticed this man scrutinizing me with his cold black eyes. Once, on a Saturday when I was closing the tanning salon I owned, I noticed him in the parking lot and he whistled at me.

Another occasion I had taken the kids to the neighborhood public swimming pool and suddenly this man showed up. He tried to have a conversation with me, but I would not engage with him. There was something very dark about him that scared me. I was simply not interested.

The man brought my attention back to the present with, "my name is Michael. I am here to take you with me. You are going to be my wife."

"Are you crazy? I don't even know you. I'm not going to marry you! What are you thinking?"

"Oh yes you are! The angels brought you to me. You are mine." Michael pushed me over to the counter where my telephone answering machine was blinking revealing a new message. Michael played the new message.

"Who is that man on the machine? Why is he calling you?"

"He is my landlord. He is calling to find out when he can bring me a new microwave. The other one stopped working. It's nothing." I could see from Michael's reactive manner that he was the jealous type. I needed to get away from this guy as quickly as possible.

"Michael, I have to go to the bathroom."

"Ok! You can go."

As I walked down the hall to the bathroom, I grabbed the phone and tried to call 911. Apparently, Michael had followed me. He busted open the bathroom door. He grabbed the phone and hung it up before the call had a chance to go through.

The failed phone scenario made him mad. Suddenly, he grabbed me by the arm and shoved me back into the family room and towards the back door.

"We are leaving. I can't trust what you would do here."

As Michael dragged me by the hair through the door, I struggled and shouted as loudly as I could. "S.J., call the police and tell them I am being kidnapped!"

"S.J., if you call the cops I will kill your mom and it will be your entire fault! You'd better stay right where you are. Don't make a move!" Michael screamed with a raucous cry resembling a disembodied spirit. Keeping the knife at my throat, Michael shoved me into his car. His older car had a bench seat and I landed hard. Michael had me by the hair as he shoved me through the driver's side door.

I was so scared that my entire body was shaking. I tried kicking him. I tried to get out the passenger door. Michael was much bigger and stronger. He pulled a gun out from under the driver's seat. He held it up against my temple and told me to "Shut up and sit still!"

When he put the gun to my head, I could feel the blood totally draining out of my face. I felt faint. I thought I was going to throw up. I started asking God to give me the strength to get through this ordeal.

We drove out into a secluded wooded area and Michael parked. Michael laid the gun down it in his lap next to the knife and turned to me.

He said, "I can see the only way I am going to be able to have you is if I kill us both. Yeah, so we can be together in heaven."

"No, you can't do that. I have kids to raise."

"They will be fine. God told me that you are mine. I have to kill us both. This is the only way we can be together."

I began praying.

"Yea, though I walk through the valley of the shadow of death, I will fear no evil; for thou art with me; thy rod and thy staff they comfort me."

God, Mary (my Guardian Angel), please protect me and help me get out of this mess! Tell me what to say and what to do. God, you have brought me this far in life; please help me live to raise my kids. I know I am asking a lot. I really need your help this time. I want to live. I have to raise the wonderful kids that you gave me. Help me!"

X X X

Throughout the night, my litany continued. The sun was beginning to rise on the tree-lined horizon. Eight hours had passed. I was scared, tired and had to go to the bathroom. I was grateful that so far I had been able to convince this crazy man not to kill us. I had talked all night trying to convince him to release me. I was running out of scripted angelic material. Michael's repertoire ranged from being quiet and calm to yelling and being out of control.

I implored the angelic realm to guide me. Here is what happened next.

Throughout the ordeal, I could hear my Guardian Angel, Mary, saying: "Tell him that you have to go to the bathroom. Insist that he take you home to use the bathroom. Tell him you simply cannot use public restrooms. Push for the opportunity to go home." That made sense to me. Surely the police would be there and I would be rescued. All would be well. I would follow the angelic instructions.

I straightened up in the car seat, "Michael, I really need to go to the bathroom."

"You can use that tree out there."

"No, I can't do that. Women can't use trees like you guys. Besides, it's too scary out there in the woods. Come on, Michael, please, take me home."

"No, don't be stupid! The police are probably waiting at your house for me. I will take you to the gas station on Spring Creek. It has a bathroom on the back side of the building. That way you won't be able to tell anyone what is going on and you won't be able to escape."

"I can't use a public restroom." I sobbed. "Please take me home. Look at it this way; if you really love me like you keep saying, then you have to take care of me. You have to take me home."

"Michael, I agree that we need to be together. How wonderful that the angels are helping us get to know each other. They are telling me right now that to develop our love we need to date like ordinary people."

"Really, well that's all I have ever wanted. When we date, then you will see how right we are for each other and you will marry me. But, if you are lying to me, I will come back and take your kids and kill them one by one. So, you better be telling me the truth. I know which schools your kids attend. I have been following you and the kids for a couple of months."

Michael finally conceded and drove me home. There were no police cars. Why not? There had to be at least one police car. Michael felt triumphant that no police cars were insight.

Somehow, I had convinced his sick mind to let me go in alone and for him to go home and call me later to set up our first date. I managed to convince him that this is the way it had to be if we were going to be together.

I went inside my house and S.J. was still sitting frozen in the same spot. He had not even moved an inch. I could not believe it because I had been gone over ten hours. S.J. was so traumatized that he never called the police.

I did not know what to do, so I called my girlfriend Sherry. She rushed right over. She called the police. I gave my story to the police, but did not get any comfort from them. The detectives said they would search for Michael, but not knowing where he was, they really did not have any good leads.

I was afraid to go to work and afraid to let the kids out of my sight. S.J. and Troy (my oldest child) were fighting over what had happened. Troy was blaming S.J. for not taking care of me. Troy thought S.J. should have at least called the police or called him to come home. But, S.J. did what Michael told him to do. Nothing!

It took the police close to two weeks to find Michael. I had convinced the detectives to use me as the bait to lure Michael out of hiding. Michael had been calling and wanting to set up our date. We agreed that on Friday night at 7:00 p.m. we would meet at the T.G.I. Fridays on Plano Pkwy. The police showed up and nailed him.

While this whole scenario was frightening, I was so grateful to my angels for protecting me and helping me to get through this alive. Michael was sentenced to jail for five years. He actually had a prior conviction for doing the same thing to another woman in Florida.

X X X

Now that this was over, it was time to re-focus. We all needed to put this behind us. Deep down inside of me, I realized I really did not trust men. They had only hurt me, used me, or let me down in one way or another. I wondered why God would create men that way or was it that I just seemed to attract the bad ones. Was I responsible for attracting such negativity in my life? Perhaps the answer was somehow connected to the fact that I was afraid of my own father.

I really needed to understand why this event had ever transpired in the first place. There are schools of thought suggesting that we co-create our life path with God. What did that mean? If that were true, why would I have created this scenario? It was time to find out. I had experienced other negative events as well. There must be a pattern that kept being repeated.

Going Deeper Into the Journey:
This event was one of many that I used to grow on my journey of self-awareness and discovery. If I were truly co-creating my life with God, how could I develop a better protection around me? And more importantly, what was inside of me that was creating this negative reality?

As I began to probe deeper, I realized that all the many areas of my life were interconnected and were affecting me as a whole. My negative patterns with men were just one small aspect. I realized I had my work cut out for me when I made the decision to co-create a healthier future.

I also wanted to discover what was blocking me from having all the things in life that I had always wanted? I needed to probe the depths of my inner being.

My Background:

The intent for this book is to teach you what I discovered along my journey towards inner peace.

My formal education consists of a Bachelors of Science in Nursing, a Masters in Psychology, and courses at Ph.D. level in Philosophy, specifically in Esoteric Studies. While this education did not yield specific tools on how to move from drama to peace, I did gain some valuable knowledge that gave me a foundation to begin my inner search.

My search for inner peace led me on a spiritual journey of self-discovery. First, my journey included reading lots of self-help books as well as spiritual and metaphysical books. These books opened me up to the idea of God being inside of me, not outside. I discovered that many spiritual people assumed the belief that we are in control of our life instead of our life being in control of us.

Second, I also attended numerous spiritual workshops and classes. Through these classes I learned how to trust my own intuition more. I realized I was responsible for my thoughts and my beliefs. I discovered that I needed to clean up my past in order to create my future the way I want it.

Third, the most important thing I learned on my journey was how to connect to God/the Universe and the Oneness of all in a spiritual way versus the religious beliefs I had been taught. I came to understand that I am a spiritual being in a human form. I am here to grow and teach and become closer to my Oneness with the Universe.

The spiritual workshops that I attended allowed me to study with leaders such as Dr. Tad James where I became certified in Time Line Therapy®, a Master Practitioner in Neuro-Linguistics, and certified as a Hypnotherapist.

I attended many workshops with Dr. Doreen Virtue. From my work in her sessions, I gained certification as an Angel Therapy Practitioner. I also became certified as a Medium. I received certification as a Medical Intuitive from additional workshops. I discovered that I was already very intuitive and really good at reading other people, just not myself. My goal was to listen to my own inner guidance for my life.

One of the most recent workshops I attended was with Her Holiness Sai Maa. I was invited to attend the workshop and then do before and after aura photos on the participants. It was exciting to see the difference in the development of people's aura after being in the presence of Sai Maa for a week. The pure love that I felt from Sai Maa was incredible. Through her example of love, I learned how to open my heart.

My Credo:

I have always believed in God and angels. As a child, I saw my guardian angels on a regular basis. In addition, in my counseling work, I see guardian angels around everyone. I fully believe our angels are here to guide us along our individual pathways.

I know that you just have to clear out all the old wounds and negative programs in order to raise your vibration which in turn enables you to be able to hear your angels more clearly. Raising your vibration also allows you to obtain goals at a higher level.

Along this journey of self-discovery, I learned some techniques that allowed me to heal the wounds from my past. Healing those wounds has changed my out-dated patterns and beliefs. This enabled me to re-direct my thoughts allowing me to create a wonderful present and future.

I have been able to hear, see, feel and know my angels and other spirits guides for many years now. I cannot imagine my life without their magnificent presence. The tools in this book are designed to help you heal your past in order to raise your vibration so that you can more easily connect into Universal guidance.

What You Can Expect to Find in This Book:

You will discover the importance of healing your past emotional wounds. Healing those childhood patterns and removing unwanted belief systems sets you in motions for unmasking your future. You will gain insight and uncover limiting beliefs and patterns that keep you in a destructive loop.

This book details how to help your spirit evolve from chaos into a sense of fulfillment and peace. I emerged from being a victim and grew to a place of empowerment. I give many examples of the different lessons that my clients and I have learned. Accordingly, readers may choose to learn from these experiences and use these lessons for self-empowerment.

I also identify probable lessons that many people come to earth to experience that are mentioned in Chapter 3. Later, I indicate how to take responsibility for your life patterns. Then, I share with you how to connect into your own inner guidance and discover your intuition.

Next, I give specific modalities on how to heal and grow. As a result, you may discover what your life can be like if you choose to take the time to heal and allow.

After your past has been resolved, then it is easy to create exactly what you want in life. Please enjoy the process of healing and move to a place of loving yourself and others. This process will also enable you to more effectively receive the guidance of your angels, spirit guides, and God.

Some of the techniques in this book were channeled to me from the Archangels and Masters of Light beings. Healing from my past has raised my vibrational frequency so that I am now able to manifest my desires in a very short time. Some of my desires have been manifested in just a couple of hours. Examples of these manifestations are discussed in Chapter 8, the Conclusion.

PART I:

HOW THE PAST AFFECTS
YOUR FUTURE

"Those who cannot remember the past are condemned
to repeat it."
George Santayona (1863–1952)

Chapter 1

Gaining Clarity

"When the defects of others are perceived with so much
Clarity, it is because one possesses them oneself."
Jules Renard (French Writer, 1864–1910)

The purpose of *Unmasking Your Future* is to help you discover
unresolved emotions that you may have stored inside your body.
These unresolved emotions send out a vibrational signal and that
determines what shows up in your life. For example, if you are
trying to create more money and the money never seems to show
up, it is because you have some unresolved issues that are
blocking the money from coming to you. The block could be an
unconscious belief that you do not deserve the money. Therefore,
that vibrational frequency of not deserving is the signal that you
are sending out to the universe and that is what is returned to
you – no money because of a belief of not deserving it.

In order to change your life, you would want to determine
what unresolved emotions or negative beliefs you have, whether
at a conscious or unconscious level, that are keeping you stuck.
These negative beliefs create self-sabotaging behaviors and
patterns. Also, the unresolved emotions when stored in the body
can result in dis-ease and illness.

Basically, you must clean up your past in order to create your
future the way you want it. You may think that you are fairly
positive and that you had a decent childhood. That may very well
be the case. However, if you do not have what you want in your
life, then you have some thoughts, beliefs, or negative patterns
somewhere that are keeping you for your desires. It is time now
to search the depths of your being and unmask those limiting

patterns.

Patterns and beliefs accumulated over a period of time create a limited perspective about life. Such limitations keep you stuck in a loop of negative dramas. When you can identify and understand how and why you are attracting to you the same set of circumstances again and again, you can begin to make positive changes.

Although, you can employ positive statements and use creative visualization techniques, if your subconscious beliefs are centered on a "feeling of not being good enough," then your subconscious goes against everything that you are trying to actualize with your conscious mind. Such an approach will not work. Rather, you must become aware of the destructive patterns and beliefs that you have accumulated in your life. Then you can release these negative patterns. When you do this, your conscious and subconscious mind will harmonize and blend influences so that you can focus on the positive.

For example, a client named Sue had been sexually abused in her childhood. As a young adult she is very intuitive and on a spiritual path. However, her abusive childhood issues have never been dealt with. Now, Sue has many health issue as a result of suppressing the unresolved issues of her abuse. Sue spends a lot of time focusing on what she wants in life, but is not able to actualize her dreams. When talking with Sue, I discovered that she doesn't believe she deserves to have anything good in her life. She believes she is a bad person and does not even like herself. These beliefs are the results of her abuse. Because Sue has these negative beliefs and they are so strong, she is unable to create anything positive in her life. Sue must heal the past and remove the negative beliefs before she can obtain her goals.

Getting Started:
Many of you have heard of the "Law of Attraction." Simply

stated this means that like attracts like. Others of you are familiar with the book or movie called "The Secret." "The Secret" is based on the "Law of Attraction." The movie tells you that you should just focus on what you want and you can have it.

Ancient mystics have known for thousands of years that everything is energy. Finally, quantum physicists have been able to scientifically proven that theory. The discovery basically states that your thoughts are energy. Those thoughts attract into your life everything that vibrates in alignment with your thoughts. Think about what you want and you attract it into your life. Think about what you don't want and you attract that into your life as well.

I agree with the law of attraction that what you focus on is what you get. "The Secret", however, left out a very important ingredient to be able to accomplish this feat. You must clean up your past in order to be able to receive what you want. Your conscious mind might be focused on what you want, but if you have underlying negative thoughts, fears, doubts or beliefs, you will not be able to actualize your desires.

For example, if you want a love relationship and focus on having the perfect relationship for you, according to "The Secret" you should be able to get your relationship. Unfortunately, what I have seen over the years with many of my clients is that they are not able to obtain all their desires. These clients may actualize some of their goals, but many of their goals stay allusive.

One such client, Jane, wanted so much to have a loving relationship. When I probed Jane about her thoughts, I discovered that she feared she would end up alone like her mom. Jane's fear of being alone was keeping her from pulling to her the love relationship she desired. Jane needed to let go of her fear of being alone.

Everything on this planet is a vibrational frequency. Our thoughts are also a vibration. Jane was sending out a vibration of fear of being alone and therefore, being alone is exactly what she pulled to her.

In this instance, Jane would want to release her fear of being alone like her mother. After more probing, we also discovered that Jane had a low self-esteem. Jane's father was verbally abusive and drank regularly. He died when Jane was a teenager, but not before he had time to enable Jane to have a low opinion of herself. He frequently found things wrong with Jane, just as he had done with Jane's mom.

The unresolved emotions connected to the wounding from her father kept Jane from finding the loving relationship she was searching for. The unresolved emotions that Jane harbored were low self-esteem, feelings of not being good enough, a belief that 'there must be something wrong with me' otherwise dad would love me, and fear of her dad. Jane knew she had these emotions stuffed deep inside, but she was not aware of the fact that these unresolved emotions were the culprit in keeping her from finding the love relationship she craved.

These negative emotions that Jane stored deep within her continued to send out vibrational signals that brought back to her more of the same abuse that Jane had received from her father. This is how "like attracts like" works. Jane had boyfriends over the years that treated her exactly like her father had treated her.

Jane saw "The Secret" and a year later sought me out to help her discover why "The Secret" was not working for her. Now that Jane and I had explored all the negative emotions and beliefs that she had about herself, she can now begin to heal and then "The Secret" will work for her.

It is important to unmask your past in order to create or actualize your future. The next several chapters will help you to uncover possible negative emotions that you have stored inside of you.

Thoughts:

Many people try very hard to be positive thinkers; however, society breeds fear and negativity. It is time now to really pay attention to your thoughts. If you have any negative or fear based thoughts, that is just enough to keep you from obtaining your desires. It takes time and practice to change your thinking so that it is focused on what you want instead of what you don't want or don't have. Most people focus on what they don't want and that is what they end up getting.

Keep your focus on what you want. Release thoughts regarding what you do not want. You will want to look at the fears associated with what you do not want. Many times people are moving away from what they don't want, only to create it. Instead, you want to move towards what you do want.

The journey of healing from your past will help you unmask your future. This process takes time, but is well worth the effort.

Chapter 2

Identifying Patterns & Beliefs

"Deal with the faults of others as gently as with your own."
Chinese Proverb

Along my journey, I discovered that inner beliefs affect your life. What you believe to be true for you creates your reality. This section will help you identify patterns and beliefs that are hindering you on your life's journey.

Many people have beliefs that have been passed down for generations. Have you taken the time to determine if those beliefs reflect what you believe to be true in your own life? Are you even aware of all the beliefs that you hold within? You will see how your beliefs create your life patterns. When you change your beliefs, your patterns will begin to change resulting in a different reality of your life.

Having had many negative events occur in my life, I decided it was time to discover what my beliefs were since they were having such an impact on my life. A belief is something that you tell yourself over and over. It is not something that is set in concrete. You can change your beliefs.

You have beliefs associated to God, religion, politics, relationships, family, children, money, career, and more. The list goes on and on. What truly are your beliefs connected to each one of these topics? What and who do you believe God is? How does God affect your life? Do you have religious beliefs that have hindered the potential for a deep-seated connection to God and your life now?

I have had several clients that possess such negative self images because of the religious beliefs that they were taught as a child. For example, one client was taught that she was such a sinner that nothing she could ever do in life would be good enough for God to love her. She had such low self-worth and low self-esteem. She could not value herself at all.

Another client was sexually abused by many of the leaders of her church all in the name of God. She has spent years working through the trauma because of her religious upbringing. She was raped and became pregnant at age 14. When she was seven months along, these wonderful leaders of the church, aborted her baby in a ritual so that they could sacrifice it to God. These religious leaders tried to convenience her that because of her sins she needed to make this sacrifice to God.

Many churches preach fear and damnation. Do you have any religious programming that is affecting your self-worth and your ability to connect to God? Do you fear God? Do you fear the possibility of going to hell? It is time to determine what your true spiritual beliefs are and how they are affecting your life.

Do you believe you deserve to have a happy loving relationship? Do you deserve to be financially secure? Are your beliefs yours, or are they someone else's beliefs? Take some time to discover what you truly believe to be true for you in all areas of your life.

In his book, *Time Line Therapy,* Dr. Tad James explains that all behaviors, patterns and beliefs are either passed down genealogically, or brought forward from past lives, or picked up from conception forward.[1] These patterns and beliefs impact every aspect of your life; therefore, it is important to discover what your beliefs and patterns are and where they originated.

Take a look at your life and determine what areas are not working for you the way you want. Do you have outdated beliefs that are keeping you feeling stuck? Do you continue to perform the same negative behaviors over and over? Let's discover your beliefs and determine which ones you no longer find useful.

HOW BELIEFS IMPACT YOUR LIFE:

Your beliefs shape the course of your life. Your belief system is the actual set of precepts from which you live your daily life. Without these precepts, you would not be able to function. Your belief system actually governs your thoughts, words, and your actions. Do you know what you believe? Do you know why you believe in the things you believe in? Review the nature of your belief system.

Beliefs can start as early as in the womb. Beliefs are really powerful things. In *Using Your Brain for a Change*, Richard Bandler says: "beliefs can compel perfectly nice people to go out and kill other human beings for an idea, and even feel good about it." [2]

Behaviors are created around your beliefs. When people make statements to you, they are reflecting their beliefs. You can assume that all behavior is expressed in direct response to your belief systems. For example, you probably would not be reading this book if you did not have a belief that the information could somehow be beneficial to you.

In *The New Peoplemaking*, Virginia Satir discusses how beliefs stem from a closed or open family system. In a closed family system, the family members are separated from outside interferences. Closed family systems evolve from certain sets of beliefs such as:

"Self-worth is secondary to power and performance.

Actions are subject to the whims of the boss.

Change is resisted."

In an open family system information is allowed to flow between the internal and external environments. The beliefs would be more like this:

"Self-worth is primary; power and performance, secondary.

Actions represent one's beliefs.

Change is welcomed and considered normal and desirable.

Communication, the system, and the rules all relate to each

other." [3]

Many of our social systems are closed including schools, prisons, churches and political groups. What about your family? Is it open or closed? Is your communication self-defeating? Are your particular rules out of date creating a closed family system? Or, is your communication growth producing and your rules up to date creating an open family system?

The purpose of knowing whether you came from a closed or open family system is to assist you in understanding whether you came from a troubled family or a nurturing family. This will help you to understand some of your beliefs and how they originated. The following is a chart from Virginia Satir's book; *The New Peoplemaking*.[4] Satir's book shows the difference between a closed system and open system.

Closed family system

Self-esteem:	low
Communication:	indirect, unclear, unspecific, incongruent, growth-impeding
Communication Styles:	blaming, placating, computing, distracting
Rules:	covert, out-of-date, inhuman rules remain fixed; people change their needs to conform to established rules
Outcome:	accidental, chaotic, destructive, inappropriate

Self-worth grows ever more doubtful and depends more heavily on other people.

Open System

Self-Esteem:	high
Communication:	direct, clear, specific, congruent, growth-producing

Communication Styles:	leveling
Rules:	overt, up-to-date, human rules; rules change when need arises
	Full freedom to comment on anything
Outcome:	related to reality; appropriate, constructive

Self-worth makes you feel more reliable and confident as you develop certain expansive growth patterns. Your self-worth, your communication skills, along with your rules and beliefs are the ingredients that comprise your family system.

Limiting Beliefs:

When you can change your belief about something, then you can change your behavior. Our beliefs drive our behaviors. Beliefs can alter and change. You believed things when you were younger that you think are silly today as an adult. For example, as a child my daughter, Sonia, believed that if a splinter went in one hand it would come out the other hand. I have no idea where she got that belief, but she refused to change her view point. Now, as an adult, of course Sonia discarded this superstitious idea.

There are things that you believe now that you never believed or thought about before. Beliefs can be very limiting or very empowering. I have a belief that for me has been very empowering. I have had this belief since I was a very little girl. I believe that I can do anything anyone else can. This particular belief empowers me because it keeps me open so that I can accumulate new data.

What beliefs do you maintain that limit you? What do you believe in and why do you believe it? Beliefs affect all areas of our life. If you want to know what your beliefs are, just watch your actions. Pay particular attention to the way you treat yourself and others. Be honest with yourself. Many people have a way of deceiving themselves into believing they are doing the right thing.

Next, you need to look at the reason behind why you do what you do. What motivates your actions, your words, and your thoughts? Many people have no clue what they really believe. They do not have any real beliefs of their own. Their beliefs were derived from the attitudes and thought patterns drawn from other people.

I have a belief that communicates the following: "All you have to do is show me something one time and I have it." The latter is useful to me. Through the many jobs I have had over the years, I have been able to immediately grasp the new information the first time it was taught to me. When I was managing a medical clinic, I hired and trained new staff. I noticed many staff members appeared to be slow learners. I wondered why they did not learn the information the first time they heard it like I did. I discovered that they did not have the same belief system. In fact, many of the new job candidates believed learning new information was difficult and took time.

To determine the source of my own belief system, I asked my four siblings what they believed in and why. None of them held the same belief of learning first time around. After some probing, what I discovered was that my father would say to us, "You better get this now because I am only going to tell you once."

In fact, I grew up afraid of my dad; so when he said, "You better get this," I did. Interestingly, my siblings heard my dad say the same thing, but they did not internalize the command the same way I did. Actually, my siblings tell me they learn very slowly. In fact, one of my sisters told me that she wished she had the belief of learning first time like I do.

It is time to discover what your beliefs are that are limiting you and keeping you stuck. A limiting belief is one that limits you and prevents you from having multiple choices. When you remove these limiting beliefs, it opens you up to limitless possibilities.

Unconscious Beliefs:

It is important to determine what your unconscious beliefs are. The conscious part of your brain does not store your beliefs. You conscious brain can only hold three to five thoughts at a time. Meanwhile, your unconscious part of the brain is where your beliefs are stored. Your unconscious part of the brain is the part that holds every memory. Your unconscious also runs your body. For instance, you do not consciously tell your body to blink your eyes, swallow, beat your heart, digest your food, etc. Your unconscious brain manages all this and more.

Because all memories are stored at the unconscious level, it is important to be able to access these memories to determine truth, wisdom, facts, and everything that comprises your thought system. You have access to all the unconscious memories; you just need to bring them into awareness.

All beliefs run your life and create your reality. Some people think that if you just focus on your goals long and hard enough that you will be able to actualize them. You will be able to obtain your goals as long as you do not have any contrary beliefs.

Your unconscious beliefs must to match your desires. For example, if you have a goal of receiving a million dollars but have a belief that you don't deserve that much money, then you will never actualize that goal.

Your beliefs must be congruent with your desires. One way to know if your beliefs are congruent with your desires is to ask yourself: "Is there anything blocking me from having.........?" If the answer is yes, determine what the block is and then proceed to remove that negative belief. Keep asking yourself that same question until you get a 'no.' At the end of that time, you should be able to obtain many of your goals very quickly.

If you do not reach your goals in a reasonable time frame,

then check your beliefs again. Keep probing to see if there are any incongruencies in your belief systems.

Money Beliefs:

Let's look at your beliefs about money since so many people have limiting beliefs in this area. Do you have a belief that 'you are not good enough' or a belief that you are undeserving? These beliefs will impact all areas of your life including your ability to generate income.

What are your beliefs about money? Some people believe that rich people are snobs, do you? Other people think being spiritual means they maintain a posture of poverty. Typically, such constricting beliefs are passed down from one generation to another. Are your beliefs pertaining to money your own or do they stem come from your family, society, or other sources?

For many years, I struggled with a lack of money. I would start a business and move towards becoming successful and later lose everything. It took two businesses and lots of financial loss before I learned that my beliefs, conscious and unconscious, were the factors that were wreaking havoc in my financial life.

After my financial setbacks, I re-evaluated my beliefs about money. I searched for the origins of my belief system. How had my parents shaped my financial belief system?

I discovered that while I was in my mother's womb I absorbed my father's beliefs about women and money. I remember my dad saying: "A woman cannot be successful without a man's help. Women do not have the ability to make as much money as men. It takes a man to make the money."

As I recalled those limiting beliefs that my father had expressed, I recognized how I was playing them out. I would become successful in my business and then for some unknown reason, I would loose everything. I did this negative pattern in two separate businesses I owned. I was single through the years of owning those businesses. My unconscious mind (the part of your brain that stores all your memories and beliefs), stored the limiting belief that I had to have a man to be successful. Recognizing that I did not have a man in my life, I would unconsciously sabotage my business and failure followed quickly. Through Time Line Therapy ®, I discovered that I had many limiting beliefs that I picked up while in my mother's womb. I noticed that I could see, hear, and feel everything that went on while I was in utero. In addition, I discovered many decisions and behaviors were also assumed during this period. I was finally able to understand why I had beliefs I was not even aware of.

I realized I had other limiting beliefs such as: Money doesn't grow on trees, nothing is free, and you have to work hard for everything, if it is too easy, there is something wrong with it, women can never be successful, men are more financially stable, women do not know how to handle money, and the list continues. Make a list of your limiting beliefs about money.

Many people have self-worth issues attached to financial stability. I have had clients that attach self-esteem and lack of self-worth to money issues as well. Do you have a belief that you are not good enough to have all the money you want? Do you self-sabotage your business dealings?

To find out more about how you feel towards money, pull a dollar bill out of your pocket. Look at it for a while. Ask the dollar bill, "How do I treat you?" Further ask, "How do I feel about you?"

Write down whatever comes to mind. Does this exercise give you any insights as to what you believe about money? Are there any negative feelings you harbor towards money? Do you just not care about money? Do you think money is a bad aspect of life? Are you afraid of money's power? Has lack of financial stability hurt you in the past?

What other views do you believe about money? When you're paying your bills, what thoughts run through your head? Are you worrying about how you are going to come up with enough money to pay your bills? Negative thinking will create that type of reality. In other words, you will not create positive thoughts about having enough money to pay your bills if you have fear and worry around it.

Instead, you should think about how wonderful your house is and how grateful you are to have such a wonderful home. This helps to create a positive reality. Being grateful for all that you have creates an abundant consciousness. This type of thinking will increase your financial abundance. Having trust and faith that God will supply everything you want will bring that reality into your life.

If your goal is to have more money and the money does not show up, then you want to look at what you are feeling inside your body. Because we store unresolved emotions in our body, you will be able to feel these emotions. Do you carry "lack of" beliefs? Do you have a belief that you never have enough money? Is your belief from this life time or a past life time? You must find the root cause of your belief. (More on the root cause and past lives later.)

For example, if your house payment is due in a week and you cannot see where the money is going to come from, you might have fear in your belly. It is hard to bring money to you when you are focused on the fear or the lack of money. The fear is probably connected to a belief that is limiting.

You would want to consider what beliefs you have that are creating the fear of not having the money for your house payment. Do you have a belief that you don't deserve your nice house? Do you have a belief that you are not good enough to have the money? Do you have a belief that you need a college degree to make more money? Do you just believe you don't deserve to make more money? Are you caught up in listening to the news and fear the nation's economy will affect you? Remember, bad news sells, good news does not. Do not get caught up in negative beliefs about the economy. Focus on what you want to accomplish in your life.

Spend more time and get to the root of your limiting beliefs. When your limiting beliefs are cleared out completely, you will be able to visualize your goal and then begin to actualize it. There is an exercise at the end of this section to help you replace old beliefs with energizing self-actualizing patterns.

Trust:
Finally, you want to make sure you trust in God to supply your needs. All you have to do is ask and be open to receive. The 'how to' is up to God. Many people get hung up on exactly how they are going to receive the money. That is not your job. Your job is to ask, trust, and to be open to receiving.

Last summer, I was scheduled to take a Grand Mediterranean Cruise with my mother and my daughter. I had already purchased the cruise and my airline ticket. Then, I experienced a large financial loss and no longer had the funds to be able to enjoy the excursions at the different ports we visited.

I prayed.

"God, please provide my $1,000 spending money for the excursions for this cruise. Everything fell into place for me to take the cruise. Now I am asking for $1,000 to enjoy the many different excursions. Thank you, God."

I asked God for the money and then let it go. The next day, my mother called and said, "I have the feeling that you are a little short on money. Do you need me to loan you some money?"

"Thanks Mom, I am a little short because my refrigerator just broke and I had to purchase a new one. I would really appreciate it if I could borrow a $1,000."

Later that same day, my daughter called saying she had a feeling I needed money. I asked and trusted that God would provide. I left the 'how God was going to provide' up to God.

Another example is demonstrated by the following story based on Peggy's limiting belief system. One of my clients, Peggy, was at a monthly group that I lead. At the April group session, I taught everyone how to manifest and create positive outcomes. I asked each group member to pick one thing that they wanted to manifest. Each person spent time visualizing one particular item that they wanted. During the meditational visualization, once they could feel their desire in their hearts, I instructed them to let it go. Trust that God will provide. Do not get caught up in beliefs about how God will provide for you. Let Spirit manifest your desires in whatever way Spirit wants. Let go of the outcome.

The following month at our group session, Peggy could hardly wait to share what had occurred. Peggy excitedly announced, "I manifested a car and it happened!"

"Peggy, that is wonderful. Tell me more." I felt so exhilarated for Peggy's joy.

"Last month you walked us through a series of steps you use to manifest and co-create. I followed your instructions. My goal was to purchase a new car. Honestly, I didn't see how I would be able to obtain the new car because my credit score is very low. I had been through a couple of hurricanes in Florida that had ruined my credit rating."

"Peggy, how did you co-create the car if you feared not being able to get financial approval?"

"Judy, you helped me with that. Financial institutes had previously rejected me. I believe you showed me how my fear of being rejected was impacting the outcome. You showed me how to get rid of the fear. The last step in the creating process is to let go, let God. In the past, I had never let go. I had always tried to figure out how I could make things happen the way I wanted them to."

"Peggy, it sounds like you did a wonderful job."

"You showed me how I was focusing on what I didn't want to

happen. That is why I often failed. I learned to focus on what I want. Thank goodness I learned a new positive program that gets great results!"

Below are the steps for creating your goals.

Steps for Manifesting Your Dreams:

1. *Write your desire down. Be very clear and specific about what you want.*
2. *Make sure your goal is focused on what you want, not what you don't want or don't have.*
3. *What is the last thing in your goal that lets you know you have it?*
4. *Put your goal into a picture.*
5. *Make sure the picture feels just right so that you see and feel yourself getting your goal. Fine tune it like you would a television set.*
6. *Now put the picture of you having this goal inside a crystal ball.*
7. *Fill the crystal ball up with the color gold.*
8. *On the outside of the crystal ball write the date you want your goal by and also write 'this or something better.'*
9. *Make a duplicate copy of the crystal ball.*
10. *Throw one crystal ball up into God's hands (or out into the universe). Put the second crystal ball out into your future where you know that date is.*
11. *Let go. The "how to" is up to God. Trust.*

Here is an example of a specific goal that I created. In 2005, I was about to go through a divorce. Michael, my ex-husband, decided it was too difficult for him to deal with a divorce and find a new home at the same time. Therefore, he bought my share of the house we owned.

I needed to create a new house for myself. It was August 22, 2005 when my daughter, Sonia, and I were sitting in a hotel room in Grand Junction, Colorado. I was taking aura photos at a Metaphysical Fair for the weekend. Sonia had recently undergone a surgical procedure and I was taking care of her.

I decided to begin my list of what I wanted in a house. I wrote down a list of everything I wanted. My desires included: a fairly new two-story home with a beautifully landscaped yard, a sprinkler system, a large storage shed in the back yard, four-bedrooms, three baths, a formal living room and dining room. I wanted lots of big windows which would make the house bright and light. I knew I wanted a humidifier connected to the furnace and, of course, air-conditioning. I wanted the house to be situated in a nice quite, safe neighborhood on a cul-de-sac. However, when I got to the basement, I wasn't clear about what I wanted. Did I want it finished or unfinished? I couldn't seem to decide on the details of what the basement would look like if it were finished, so I put a question mark next to finished or unfinished basement on my inventory sheet.

After writing my wish list, I visualized a crystal ball. I saw myself inside the crystal ball marking everything off my list. I took the time to feel the excitement of receiving all I wanted.

Next, I filled the crystal ball up with gold sparkles. I used gold because it is a very high vibrational color. It is the color my angels have instructed me to use. Then I wrote the date of September 15, 2005 on the outside of the ball. I wanted my house by this date. Under the date I wrote: "This or something better."

Next, I made a duplicate copy of the crystal ball. I visualized myself tossing one crystal ball up through the sun and into God's hands. (I pretended I could see God's hands waiting to receive my crystal ball.) Then, I visualized placing the second crystal ball out in front of me on the date of September 15, 2005.

For me, my future stands out in front of me just off to the right. You would want to determine where you feel your future might be in relationship to your body. To determine your future think of any future plans that you have and notice what direction those plans seem to lead you. Are they in front of you, off to the right, off to the left, above or below you? Perhaps your future plans are behind you. Just get a feel for where you think your future plans are. What direction would you point to if you were telling me where your future is stored?

Three days after I visualized my house, I had some free time. I asked my daughter, Sonia, if she wanted to go with me to find my new home.

I backed out of my driveway and stopped. "Archangel Michael, Mary and Philip (my Guardian Angels), please tell me which direction to go to find the house that fits my requirements."

I could hear Archangel Michael telling me driving directions. About twenty-minutes later and while receiving Michael's directions the entire time, we pulled into a cul-de-sac. The first house on the right had a for sale sign.

"Wow Mom, there's a house for sale!" Sonia seemed to be in shock. She hopped out of the car and grabbed the flyer out of the little box. Sonia compared the flyer up with my wish list.

Everything on the list matched. My bonus was a beautiful lake situated across the street. My limited creativity didn't think of the lake, that is why I always write, "this or something better" to allow for my limited thinking.

The house had every feature I had visualized. Of course, you must know, the basement was unfinished because I could not make up my mind about that. When you don't know what you want, you get nothing because the Universe doesn't know what to manifest without your specific instructions.

Looking back over that event, I often wonder why I wasn't sure about whether the basement should be finished or unfinished. At the time, I remember thinking I may not like the way in which the basement would be finished, which is silly, because I could have created it the way I wanted it. Apparently, it was not that important to me.

My neighborhood is beautiful and very peaceful. My house is wonderful. God gave me exactly what I asked for. My realtor was shocked when I called her and said I found the house I wanted to purchase. I hadn't even seen the inside. I knew that it was everything I had asked for. My realtor was not accustomed to working with a client like me. She tried to convince me to look at other homes, but I didn't need to. I had found my home.

Relationships:

You draw your beliefs and patterns about relationships from your family value system and conditioning. How your mom and dad treated each other while you were growing up creates your model of how to engage in meaningful relationships. The way in which your parents interact and treat you reflects how you establish your sense of self-worth.

How did your siblings treat you as you were growing up? Were you told lots of negative things repeatedly about yourself? What kind of relationship did you have with yourself? How does that impact you now? Did you lie to yourself? In the past, did you tell yourself that you did not deserve to be happy and have the things that you wanted?

Patterns of communication play a big role in developing your current belief system. If you did not develop a solid sense of self-worth as a child, it would be easy to use another's actions and reactions to define yourself. For instance, if someone called you dumb, you might agree. You might agree because someone in your environment insisted this was true.

It is easy for you to get hooked into doubts regarding your self-worth if you did not develop a positive or solid self-worth. Later, when your self-worth is challenged you internalize negative feelings. Your stomach gets knotted up, your muscles tighten, and you might start holding your breath. All of this occurs while your thoughts reveal the following: "Who cares about me, I'm dumb? I am unlovable. I never do anything right."

This creates feelings of anxiety, incompetence, fear, helplessness, or embarrassment. All of these feelings are stored deep within our bodies. Based on the patterns from childhood you might feel you need to make things right with the person that called you dumb. You may think you have to say and do whatever you need to do in order to receive their approval. You think survival is in their hands. When you do this, you give your power away.

Instead, if you keep your survival and power in your own hands, you can express what you feel and think. You might worry about exposing a weakness and fear taking a bigger risk, but you avoid the greater pain of hurting yourself. You can learn to feel more worthy enabling you to speak your truth.

Patterns and belief systems that we establish in our childhood are often the ones we utilize in our adult relationships. Now it is time to evaluate them. Are you getting what you want in your relationships? Do your relationships reflect your own sense of self-worth? Are your relationships supportive and positive?

What type of relationship do you have with your mom and dad now that you are an adult? Are you following in your parents' footsteps? Are you treating your kids in the same way your parents treated you, even though you hated it as a child?

If you are a female, did you marry the same type of man as your father? Do you have the same type of relationship with your husband as your mother has with your father? I see many people that create the exact same marriage as their parents. Many of those marriages are toxic, but without realizing it, you create the exact same toxic relationship.

We attract people to us that mirror the wounds of our childhood. For example, you might marry a man that mirrors the negative behaviors of both your parents. Sometimes, you only marry a partner that mirrors the most negative of parental patterns. Then, you attract additional negative patterns as reflected by your parents in the form of bosses, co-workers, and friends. How can we avoid such self-defeating patterns?

As a child you are probably going to get wounded in some respect. These wounds are negative emotions that you typically store inside your bodies. These wounds then act as little stressors. As you grow, these little stressors serve as triggers for your emotions. Other people can press your negative triggers all too easily. Having your triggers pushed is an opportunity for you to see the negative emotions that you have stored inside your body. Then, you can begin to heal them. When you think about this lesson, it is really wonderful how the universe brings to you people that mirror all your negative emotions. Thus you are given this great opportunity to heal negative beliefs and patterns.

Changing Beliefs:

A belief is just something that you have told yourself over and over. To change or remove a belief that no longer serves you, go to the root cause (the first time) you made the decision to have that belief.

Beliefs and patterns are changeable. When you change your beliefs, then you can also change your range of patterns. Below is an exercise to help you change the beliefs that you no longer want or find appropriate.

The best way to change a belief is to go to a NLP practitioner. He or she can help you discover why you persist in hanging on to the outdated beliefs you have. The NLP Practitioner can suggest ways to help in the reprogramming process. However, the following is a general overview of how to change a belief.

Think of a belief about yourself that you would like to be different. This should be a belief that limits you in some way. I want you to think of that belief that you would rather not have. Put that belief aside for a moment.

Now, I want you to think of something you are doubtful about. It might be true, or it might not be. Next, I want you to notice how those two experiences of belief and doubt are different. Is your belief a big picture or small? It is bright, vivid and detailed. Or is the picture small, dim and fuzzy? Does it fill up the entire frame or is there little room for the background.

This is much like adjusting your T.V. set. What is the picture like? Notice the differences. Now, take the list of differences and test them one at a time in order to find out which ones are the most powerful in changing your belief.

For example, take your picture of belief and try making it smaller. Does that change it to doubt? If not, take the bright and vividness and change it to dim and drab. Does that change your belief to doubt?

If not, take the detailed picture and make it blurry. Then, go to a stable picture and make it flash. Next, try a framed picture and then go to no frame. Then, try little background to lots of background. Is the picture right in front of you or off to the side?

One of these modalities is going to change your belief to one of doubt.

First, start thinking about your belief now and be sure you think about it in positive terms. Think of what you want to believe, not what you don't want to believe.

Second, I want you to frame that belief in terms of a process or ability that would result in you getting that goal.

Third, I want you to take some time to imagine how you would act differently if you already had this new belief. Think of any ways in which this change could be a problem for you, or the people who are close to you. If you can't think of any way that this new belief could be a problem, then that is your new belief. Set this new belief aside for a moment.

Fourth, I want you to take that big picture of the belief you do not like and move it all the way over to where your doubt is. As you do that, the picture will lose its frame and get dimmer, small, and blurry and start flashing. When that picture flashes off, have the picture of the old belief disappear, and then have the picture of the *new belief flash back on.*

Fifth, take the picture of your new belief and move it back to the center of your visual field. As you do this, notice how it develops a frame and gets bigger, brighter, sharper and more vivid.

Richard Bandler goes into detail about how to change your beliefs in his book, *Using Your Brain for a Change.* [5]

THE CYCLE OF LIFE

Basic patterns stem from three different periods in our life. The first consists of the **Imprint Period**, where a child is like a sponge. The child soaks up all the sights, sounds, feelings, tastes, and smells that occur in his/her life. The **Imprint Period** spans the years from approximately birth to age 7. Between the ages of 8 to 13 comes the **Modeling Period**. This period demonstrates how a child models its parents' behavior and other major figures in its life. Next, is the **Socialization Period** that occupies ages 14 to 21. This period spans the gap when teens go outside the family and meet other significant people. Social values are created during this period. [6]

These three periods are stages in which we develop our patterns, beliefs and behaviors. To discover the negative patterns that you currently posses, you can start with your birth family or your adopted family. All events that occur from the time of conception forward, at some level, have meaning. Using hypnosis to regress adults to the time of conception validates these conclusions. Many times, infants take on limiting beliefs and negative behaviors while still in the womb. In some cases, the limiting beliefs are without any additional context that could adequately explain them. Later, without understanding all of the circumstances, these limiting beliefs become the foundation for later behaviors and false belief systems.

For example, let's say your mom is experiencing depression during her pregnancy. While you are in the womb, you can feel and sense your mom's depression. Out of love, you might choose to assume the same feelings of depression thinking that you are relieving your mother of her depression. In the womb, you do not have the conscious ability to recognize that you cannot take the depression away from your mother. Instead, you both end up in the throws of depressive patterns. Also, as a young being in the womb, you are not able to recognize that your mom's depression is connected to hormonal changes. In fact, her depression may resolve once the pregnancy is completed and her hormones return to normal levels.

You may also assume negative beliefs, patterns, and behaviors at an early age. For example, let's say you are five years old and see a toy at the store that you want, but your mother says "no." You can take that 'no' and internalize it to mean: "I never get what I want, Mom doesn't love me! Something is wrong with me for even wanting that toy."

Without understanding what is really going on in Mom's head, you do not know the real reason why you were told 'no.' Here, you are taking the issue out of context and registering it without full understanding. The simple reason might have been that Mom was in a hurry. Perhaps, she did not want to take the time for you to buy the toy. Of course, the possible beliefs that you internalized from that scenario may affect future events.

There are many behavioral patterns that we pick up from our parents. Here is a list of several probable sources of parental conditioning:

- Addictions
- Blaming others
- Eating disorders
- Trust issues
- Insecurity
- Neat or sloppy
- Fears

- Playing the Victim
- Anxieties
- Relationship patterns
- Money patterns - over spending, being too tight, fear of money

Determine where your patterns originated. Let's start with mom and look at the patterns you modeled from her or wounds that were created because of her behaviors.

Mom's Patterns:
While in the womb, you feel, hear, and know everything that is going on around you. At this point, you are able to assume your ancestors' patterns, beliefs and behaviors. Many people absorb their mother's emotions while in the womb. Some people absorb these emotions in the hopes of taking the negative emotions away from Mom only to find out later on that both share the same negative emotions.

Jessica's Story:
One client named Jessica came to me because of her experience of depression. Jessica has sad brown eyes and long dark hair. I used a process called Time Line Therapy® on her. During this process Jessica discovered that her depression began while she was in the womb. In fact, her mom had depression during the pregnancy. Jessica held the belief that she could help her mom by taking on the pattern of depression. Unfortunately, this is not true. Both Jessica and her mom ended up suffering from depression.

Time Line Therapy® is a process that I am certified to use. I studied this process with Dr. Tad James. This particular healing modality allows you to go back into your past in a dis-associated state. In this way you can learn to change the emotional trigger associated with a specific event and release limiting decisions.

In this scenario, Jessica had made a limiting decision to be depressed that began in her mom's womb. Regressing Jessica back to the womb, she was able to see that the depression was really her mom's and not hers. Through the healing process, Jessica was able to release the decision to be depressed. Thus, she was able to change the emotionally charged negative outcome.

Sue's Sabotage:

Sue, a petite redhead, came for help because she reflected patterns of self-sabotage. We discovered that Sue carried the same sabotaging patterns of her parents. Sue picked up this particular pattern while in the womb. In fact, Sue discovered that the pattern had been passed down for several generations. Later, Sue discovered many other patterns that she had absorbed while in utero. Such patterns include victim and abandonment. Sue also reflected beliefs pertaining to issues of not being good enough, low self-esteem, and low self-worth.

Sue could finally understand where her limiting patterns had originated. She was able to draw insights from her parents' comments and behaviors to her own limiting beliefs. Sue realized that she unconsciously sabotaged herself to the point that she could not surpass her mother's level of growth. She uncovered the knowledge that her mom had held dreams that remained unfulfilled when Mom became pregnant.

Sue's mom, Marilyn, never really wanted a child. Marilyn wanted a career as an artist. When Marilyn became pregnant out of wedlock, she was forced to give up her dreams of art school. Instead, she was forced to go to work. Sue's dad abandoned Marilyn as soon as he found out about the pregnancy. A few years later, Marilyn married Sue's step-dad.

Sue felt abandoned by both her mom and birth dad. Marilyn never seemed to be there emotionally for Sue. Now Sue understood what had happened. Sue felt a need to punish herself for disrupting her mom's initial dreams. Sue never felt good enough. She believed that if her mom had been better to her dad, he would have never left her. What Sue didn't know growing up was that her dad left because of his inability to take responsibility. His leaving was not about Sue.

Sue could finally see all of this and begin the healing process. This session was very enlightening for her. Sue was ready to stop punishing herself for her what had been her parents' choices.

Anxious Terry:

Terry, a twenty-six year old, sought me out due to anxiety he was experiencing. Terry is a tall nice looking man. He appeared nervous with a constant leg twitching.

"Terry, what are you so anxious about?" I asked scanning his restless body.

"I am anxious about everything. It is so bad I have not been able to work for the last two years. I get so nervous just leaving the house. I can't seem to cope with anything."

"I know it took a lot of courage just to come here today, Terry. Let's see if we can get to the root of your anxiety. How long have you been feeling this type of anxiety?"

"I can't remember ever not feeling some level of anxiety." He said as he sat with his legs crossed. Terry's top leg moved with increased intensity.

I gained a little more history from Terry. Terry explained that he meditates regularly and feels he knows himself quite well. He just wanted to learn how to remove the anxiety so he could feel comfortable leaving the house and getting a job.

We discovered that he picked up his anxiety after he was born. His mom was anxious about being a new mother. Terry could feel her anxiety. Terry's mom felt anxious about many other things as well. Terry could feel his mom's anxiety and began internalizing it. Terry did not work because he felt too stressed and anxious to do so.

This session was enlightening to Terry. After discovering the core reason for his anxiety, I taught him some techniques on how to remove the anxiety out of his body. Those techniques are discussed later in this book.

Guilt Monger:

Another client, Cindy, recently called for an appointment. She explained, "My mom often makes me feel guilty about many things in my life."

Cindy is a short heavy set woman with intense large brown eyes. I could see that she was very upset over her mother's constant complaints about her life.

"My mom insists that I call her daily. This frustrates me. Mom projects heavy guilt trips on me when I don't call her everyday. My mom says that a good daughter would want to call her mom every day to check on her. Well, obviously I am not a good daughter. I just don't want to talk to her so often. Mom is so negative that I feel so awful when I am done talking to her. It takes me hours to shake her negativity. What do I do?"

"Cindy, how long has your mom treated you this way?"

"Mom has treated me this way my whole life. Mom also insists that I visit her every Sunday. I have developed feelings of resentment towards my mom because of the guilt she puts on me when I don't abide by her wishes."

I taught Cindy the 'Roll Up' technique that is detailed later in this book. Being able to "roll up" her mom's energy, Cindy was able to rid herself of the negative feelings. Because of utilizing the "roll up" method, Cindy felt so much relief releasing many of the pent-up frustrations.

Harboring Feelings:

Does your mom or someone else in your family try to make you feel guilty? Do you harbor feelings of resentment towards a specific family member? What feelings are you holding onto that are blocking you from enjoying a happy fulfilled life?

Modeling:

In the book, *Human Development Across the Lifespan,* authors John Dacey and John Travers mention that girls take on the roles and patterns of their mothers. Boys appear to do the same thing with their fathers. This book illustrates how many fathers tend not to play an active role in their children's lives. This fact affects the attachment theory and behavioral patterns that children have. [7]

For example, if your mother learned to play the role of a victim, then as a girl, you might model that same role. You might then continue to play the victim in your adult life. In addition, if your mother acted as a caregiver to your father and other members of the family, then chances are, as a girl, you learned the same pattern of behavior.

Review your behaviors and patterns and determine which ones you model after your mother. Notice if these behaviors serve as useful patterns. Playing the role of a victim is not a useful pattern and one that you might want to consider changing.

Another possible pattern you might have modeled from your mother could be the need for self-punishment and self-sabotage. These patterns are indicative of a low self-esteem or feelings of not being worthy.

Perhaps your mother was the peacemaker of the family. Are you the peacemaker of your family? Do you feel it is your job to see to it that every one gets along? If family members are fighting, do you intervene attempt to resolve the issues?

In the past, many generations of women have carried on the "suffer in silence" syndrome. These women have gone through life never having the chance to speak their truth. Many of them have maintained the belief that somehow they were subservient to men. These women reflected to each subsequent generation that doing anything for themselves was a selfish consideration. Do you feel guilty about taking time for yourself? Is it hard for you to give time and space to yourself? Do you have a hard time receiving? If so, it is time to change all of those negative belief systems, behaviors, and patterns. It's time to learn to love yourself. If you can't love yourself, how can you expect others to love you?

Dad Patterns:

What patterns are associated with your father that has hindered your development? Have you assumed some of the same patterns and behaviors that your father has demonstrated to you over the course of your life? Was your father emotionally absent while you were growing up? Did he help create a pattern of emotional abandonment that you replay in your life today?

Was your father unable to give you love, understanding, or approval? Many people spend years as over-achievers because they are waiting to get their father's approval. Are you one of these people?

Was your father domineering and controlling? As an adult, have you become the same way? Many times, parents are so controlling that the child feels they have no control over their lives. When they become an adult, they become very controlling in order to make up for not having had feelings of freedom or self-expression in the past.

Elizabeth's Father:

Elizabeth, a 38-year-old client, came to me upset because of her controlling boss. I knew that her controlling boss was mirroring back old wounds from her childhood. In the past, she had experienced the impact of having a controlling father. She mentioned that she still gets angry whenever her dad tells her what to do.

Elizabeth has not healed the original wounds that were created as a child when she was connected to her controlling father. If she had healed these wounds, she would no longer be attracting controlling people around her in her current environment.

I explained to Elizabeth that we all have negative experiences in our childhood that leave us somewhat "wounded." Until these wounds are healed, we keep attracting people to us that match those original wounds. It is important to see these experiences as opportunities to heal.

It is really great how the Universe sets life in motion. The Universe tries to assist us in learning the lessons we came here to learn. We pick our parents to set up the learning loops and then the hope is to eventually learn the lessons and move towards healing and complete unconditional forgiveness.

It is great when you can look at everyone as mirroring your own issue. Everyone in your life reflects the good and bad about you. The bad things are the wounds from your childhood that you have not yet healed. This is great because the universe gives you a lot of chances to see these wounds with all the people that are presented in your life.

Elizabeth could see how she had attracted some friends and co-workers that mirrored for her the controlling behavior of her father.

"Wow, this is exciting! I see I can begin to heal many wounds just by looking at the things that push my buttons. When I am with my friends and co-workers, I can learn a lot of valuable life lessons. Thanks, Judy. I am excited to get started."

Dad Doesn't Love Me:
Amy, a 42-year-old client, came to me because she still had not found Mr. Right. Amy is a fairly attractive woman. She is very tall, reaching almost six feet. Even though Amy carries herself confidently, she expressed how insecure she felt when it came to relationships.

Our work uncovered childhood patterns associated with not feeling good enough. Her dad was not there emotionally for her in many ways. She internalized that to mean something was wrong with her.

"I have never felt that Dad loved me. I always felt that I must be unlovable." Amy harbored these beliefs about herself at an unconscious level.

"Amy, do you suppose that you are unconsciously sending out negative vibes because you feel unlovable and believed that you are not good enough? Do you think that you are attracting men to you that treat you badly because you feel bad about yourself? Can you see how you are attracting these negative men to you? Is it possible that they support your unconscious belief that you are not worthy of being loved?"

"Yes, I think I am seeing how I attract these negative men. I guess I have always felt that if my own dad couldn't love me, then how could someone else ever think of doing the same."

Childhood Wounds:
Numerous client revelations show me that many times girls over-develop their masculine side to over compensate in order to get their father's attention and approval. In other words, they become more like their dad instead of modeling their mom's behavior.

I also believe that we develop wounds in our childhood that are associated with our parents. We store those wounds holographically in our body. These wounds are comprised of negative beliefs and unresolved emotions. They include: anger, fear, guilt, sadness, hurt, and disappointment. Later, these unresolved emotions send out a vibrational frequency. Such emotions are attracted back to you mirroring the vibration of what you are sending out.

Are you attracting partners that reflect the negative aspects of your parents? There is an old saying that women marry their fathers and men marry their mothers. We attract partners that mirror the wounds of both parents. In some insistences, girls may appear to 'marry their father' because there are more unresolved emotions connected to dad. However, if you look hard enough, I believe that you will find your partner possesses many of the emotional wounds that you retain from both parents. We also attract the good aspect of our parents to us. Therefore, many times we attract a partner that mirrors the positive aspects of our parents as well.

Mirrors:

My client, Sarah, married a man that mirrored all the exact patterns and behaviors that she did not like in her mother. Sarah married Tom at a young age of nineteen. At that time, Sarah thought Tom was perfect. Later, Sarah realized that Tom possessed many of the same qualities of her mother.

Sarah's mom was emotionally detached from her and so was Sarah's husband. Sarah's mom was very critical of Sarah and so was her husband. The negative behaviors that Sarah's mom expressed when Sarah was a child created deep emotional wounds.

Because Sarah did not know as a child how to deal with her feelings, the latter caused emotional wounds to be stored within her body. On an unconscious level, Sarah sent out the vibes of emotional detachment and criticism, which resulted in her attracting other people that stayed detached from her and criticized her.

See if you have patterns that you have repeated in the different relationships you have been in. These negative patterns reveal themselves in bosses, friends, co-workers, and neighbors.

Find the Core Issue:

Look deep within and see if you are carrying any anger, hurt, sadness, resentment, pain, rejection, sorrow, anxiety, stress, jealousy and fear. Identify the source of these emotional attachments. Some feelings may be connected to siblings. However, other feelings might be linked to other relatives, friends, and spouses. Create an inventory of all the negative emotions that you are ready to release. Notice how the patterns have been set up. Trace each one of the patterns through your life up to the present.

Most wounding starts either in past lives, or is created in the womb. Such wounding can also be passed down genealogically, or stem from the first ten years of your life. Many times, people do not remember particular childhood events because the unconscious mind suppresses negative memories. Your unconscious mind suppresses memories as a way to help you survive even the most taxing and difficult situations.

However, it is important to be able get to the root cause of the wound. Do your best to remember your past and find the core issue of the unresolved emotions. Some past memories can be very traumatic. Thus, when searching for the root cause, if you should you come across a traumatic event; you might need professional help to sort through the conflicting emotions. One way to assist you is to remain disassociated from the event. This will help you to look at the event without being attached to the emotions of the event.

Disassociation means to be disconnected. If you view a past memory like you are watching it on television, you are disassociated from the emotions of the event. You can see the event is connected to you, but you do not feel the emotions as strongly.

When you are associated into an event, you are feeling the emotions strongly in your body. This can cause you to re-live the experience. While trying to heal past negative experiences, it is easier to disassociate from the emotions in order to gain a broader perspective of the event and the lessons. You do not need to re-live the trauma in order to heal. You want to identify the negative emotions and gain an understanding of what the lesson is that you are learning.

As you discover what the unwanted emotions are, you will want to pull them out of your body. We tend to store unwanted emotions in various parts of our body. When you are a child and hold emotional experiences inside, you pay for it as an adult through illness and unhappiness.

Here is an example of how to find the core event and release the negative emotions attached to it.

Let's say that you decide to remove the pattern and negative emotion of fear around not having enough money. You start by discovering the first time you made the decision to have fear about not having enough money. You want to go to the first time you felt fear. If you only went back to last week when you felt fear, you would not be removing the pattern. You would only be deflecting the energy off that one event. When healing, clearing, or removing patterns, beliefs, or negative emotions, you must go to the core even, the root cause.

In order to find the root cause, you simply ask yourself:

"What is the root cause, the first time I made the decision to have fear about not having enough money?"

Continuing asking yourself, "Was the root cause before, during, or after birth?" The first thing that comes to mind is the correct answer.

If your answer is after birth, ask, "At what age?"

If your answer is before birth, then ask, "Was it in the womb or before?" If your answer is in the womb, then ask, "How many months along?"

If your answer is before, then ask, "Passed down genealogically or in past lives?" If your answer is past lives, then ask, "How many life times back?"

If your answer is passed down genealogically then ask, "mother's side or father's side." After determining the side of the family it is on, ask, "How many generations back?"

Now that you have determined the root cause, you want to go back to that time. You will need to discover where you store your past memories. As you think about your past, begin to notice in what direction those memories come to you from. As you think back, what was the name of the college that you attended, the name and location of your high school, and what was the name of your junior high school? As these memories come to you, notice what direction they are coming to you from. Are they coming from behind you, in front of you, off to the left, off to the right, above you, or inside your body somewhere? Just notice the direction as you think about your past memories. There is no right or wrong direction.

Your present is where you are right now. Next, let's discover your future. Think about any future plans that you might have. What direction do those memories come to you from? Are those memories out in front of you, above you, off to the right, off to the left, behind you, or somewhere inside your body?

Notice how your past is connected to your present, and then connected to your future. This is known as your Time Line. Now, take in a few deep breaths and float way up in the air. Go ahead and go way up high above all your memories. Float all the way back into the past. You will either see, hear, feel, or sense all those memories down below. Just get a feel or sense of them.

Now, turn around so that you are facing the present and begin to come along your time line towards now. Notice if you have any dark spots or empty holes in your time line. Perhaps your past feels or looks the same to you.

Next, zoom all the way out into the future. Go all the way out to the very end of your future. Turn around and come back to now. What do you notice? Does your time line all look the same or notice that your future looks brighter than your past?

Now that you have discovered your time line, it is time to go back to the root cause of your fear of lack of money. This would be considered a limiting decision with the negative emotion of fear attached to the decision. It is a limiting decision because it limits you from feeling positive or neutral about money.

Ask yourself, "What is the root cause the first time I made the decision that there is not enough money?" The first thing that comes to mind is the answer.

In this example, it is in past lives. Next ask, "How many life times back?" If you answer, "I don't know," then continue with: "I know you don't know, but if you did know how many life times back is it?" What is your answer? Keep asking until you get the answer. Trust what comes to mind.

In this example, we will go with ten life times back. So, float all the way up in the air and go all the way back into the past ten life times until you can see, hear, feel, or sense that life time is directly below you now.

Noticing that event below you, what are the negative emotions attached to that event? The event is not important, but if you can see or sense what the event is that is fine. The emotions attached to the event are what you are looking for.

Next, ask what the positive lesson is around that particular event. In this example case, the lesson is trusting that the universe will provide. Now you want to save or store the positive lessons in the special place that you store all such positive lessons. That is a special place in your brain that your unconscious knows. If you do not get a positive lesson, that is okay, because your unconscious mind always knows the lesson.

Next, go back into your past twenty minutes before that event occurred. Turn around and face the present. Now, where are the negative emotions? They should have disappeared. If not, go back into your past a little more and float a little bit higher until the emotions disappear.

Once the emotions are gone, come back along your time line towards now only as quickly as you can allowing all those emotions to disappear as an issue in your life. Notice how all the events re-evaluate themselves in complete support of you now trusting that the universe will provide for you.

Once you are back to the present, where in your body did you store all those negative emotions? Where in your body did you store the belief that there is not enough money? Take your hand and pull all of those emotions out of your body along with the limiting belief. (If you need a reminder on how to pull the energy out of your body, *please review the Technique for Releasing Negative Emotions in Chapter 1.)*

You should feel much lighter and no longer have the gnawing fearful feeling or the belief in scarcity of abundance pertaining to money.

*If you have had a lot of trauma in your life, please do not do these procedures without the guidance of a trained Time Line Therapist. You can visit my website at **www.alternativechanges.com** or you can search for a certified Time Line Therapy practitioner.*

Abandonment/Victim Patterns:

Emotional Abandonment:
Many people recognize the abandonment/victim issue. Dad abandons you emotionally. Mom teaches you how to play the victim. Later, you tend to attract men that are unavailable emotionally or men that abandon you and you accede to role playing the victim.

Some of these patterns that we run have been passed down for several generations. Remember your family history. Perhaps then you will understand how some of the beliefs and patterns originated.

For example, in some families the abandonment/victim patterns began several generations back. According to history, many young families moved west to find new opportunities and start a new life. Husbands would build a house for their families. Then, the man would go off hunting for weeks at a time to obtain a supply of food for the winter.

If a frontiers woman became overwhelmed with children, tending to the homestead, or taking care of everything around the house, she might have taken on the belief of being a victim to her circumstances. She could also have felt abandoned by her husband.

Children have the tendency to pick up on the feelings of

others around them. Therefore, if mom is feeling abandoned and like a victim the children would easily assume the same feelings.

In the colonial past, women were raised to be the home makers. Fathers did not participate fully in their children's lives due to the belief that it was the woman's job to raise the children. Fathers spent more time with their sons because of the pattern of raising their sons to be men that would follow in their footsteps. They were expected to serve as hunters and protectors.

Girls would grow up feeling neglected and unloved by their fathers because more time had been given to the boys. Girls would feel abandoned by their fathers. Often girls would then internalize those feelings of inadequacy. Subsequently, young women tried to win approval, love, and attention. Did this happen in your family or in the family of anyone you know?

Some families are still running the same program where the father abandons the children emotionally and mom studiously plays the victim role. Look at the details of your life. Determine if you have any victim patterning. Are such patterns due to emotional or physical abandonment by one or both of your parents?

Discovering Abandonment/Victim Patterns:

Here is the story of how one of my clients put together her abandonment/victim patterns. She had not realized that she had been playing the victim role until I pointed it out in one of our sessions.

Janet was scheduled to go to court in January 2001. This event was the catalyst that allowed her to see how she continually played the victim role.

Here is what happened. Her oldest son had a daughter born June 5, 1999. Here was a beautiful girl named Sydney. Janet's son never married the mother of his child. When Janet's son filed for parental rights and custody, the door was opened for Janet to file for grandparent visitation.

In fact, Janet's son let Janet see Sydney whenever she wanted. However, not knowing how his visitation rights were going to turn out, Janet thought it best that she file for her individual rights of visitation. The courts granted her four hours on the third Monday of each month.

Sydney's Mom provided different excuses on many of the Mondays that Janet was scheduled to visit Sydney. In fact, what was happening was that Janet was refused visitation. After two years of many missed visits, Janet finally filed contempt of court charges against Sydney's mother, Courtney. This was the reason why she had to go to court that Friday morning in January of 2001.

Janet's husband told her that particular morning that he was not going with her to court. He said his "work schedule was more important." Janet felt abandoned. As soon as she got off the elevator at the courthouse, Courtney's attorney, Mr. Smith, cornered her. Because Janet's husband did not want Janet to spend money on an attorney, Janet had to fend for herself. The attorney, Mr. Smith, took them to a little room so that they could "work things out."

Mr. Smith stated that he would act as a mediator since Janet did not have an attorney. Once escorted in the little white conference room, Courtney immediately started yelling at Janet and calling her names. Mr. Smith did not stop Courtney from her vicious tirade and outburst.

Janet wanted to escape. This was torture for her. Two hours later, when the tirade ceased, Janet caved in. Janet dropped the charges. Because of her old subconscious patterns and beliefs that supported her victim/abandonment issues, Courtney won a victory. Janet also had succumbed to patterns of fear and insecurity when placed in confrontational situations.

Angry with her son for getting Courtney pregnant and putting her in this situation, Janet left the courthouse. Janet was also furious with her husband for not supporting her in her quest for visitation. During the drive home from the courthouse, Janet called both her son and her husband. She yelled at them for what they had done to her.

A couple of hours later Janet was forced to looked within. She went from the courthouse straight to a Metaphysical Fair where she was doing Tarot readings. Janet had been at the fair for two hours and still she had no customers. Since I was working at the same Metaphysical Fair, Janet asked me to look at her energy to see why no one wanted to be near her.

I pointed out to her that she had previously been acting like a victim: "How could my son have done this to me?" "How could my husband have not been there for me, leaving me to be fed to the lions alone?" "How could Courtney be so difficult?" Janet was full of repressed fear, rage, and frustration.

The intensity of her situation hit her like a ton of bricks. Yes, she was promoting the victim pattern. She had learned this pattern from her mom. It also appeared that her husband abandoned her. In turn, this supported her belief that men were never present emotionally for her. The situation mirrored the wounds her dad had previously inflicted in her as a young girl. What an eye opener for her!

Family Patterning:
Look at your family. How would you describe it? Did you come from a troubled family? In her work, *The New Peoplemaking, Virginia Satir addresses* family dysfunctions. Satir states "that the family is a microcosm of the world." [8] To understand the world you begin by describing the family. Look at such issues as power struggles, intimacy, autonomy, trust, and communication skills. To change the behavior in the world, you have to start by changing the behavior within the family.

Physical Abandonment:
With such high divorce rates, many children experience actual

physical abandonment by a parent. In some instances one of the parents chooses to move out of state, which creates a physical abandonment. In other instances, there is so much fighting between the parents that sometimes one of the parents just walks away. This is because they no longer can cope with the degree of conflict. Such conflict can create all kinds of emotional issues in the children.

One client, Julie, shared her story with me. When Julie divorced Jim, the father of her two children, she assumed full custody of the kids. Meanwhile, Jim had visitation every other weekend. Julie told Jim that he could see the children whenever he wanted. However, visitation could not interfere with school. Eventually, Jim began to withdraw and ignore his responsibilities.

Sometimes Jim would call and tell the kids that he would pick them up on Friday right after work. Friday night would roll around; Jim would not show up. On several occasions, Jim would say that he had to work and needed to cancel the weekend visitation. This created a pattern of disappointment and triggered abandonment for the kids.

Jim worked for Julie's father's company. One occasion, Jason the oldest child, called Julie's dad, his grandfather, and asked what project could be so important that Jim had to work all weekend. Julie's dad replied, "Jim's not working this weekend. What are you talking about?" Upon receiving this news, Jason immediately became hurt, disappointed, and angry.

Both of the kids felt abandoned by their father. They both began to feel unwanted. They internalize the rejection. They were unable to discern the true reason for the recurring pattern of rejection.

Although, Jim had the right to see the kids, he chose not to. Later, Julie moved to a different state. Now, geography defined the terms of abandonment. Obviously, the kids could no longer see their father on the weekends. Jim had the right to have the kids for the summers. Most of the time, he chose not to see the kids at all.

Julie's boys are both grown now. Interestingly enough, they both have experienced relationship after relationship in which the girlfriend abandons them leaving them for another man. This pattern perpetuates the stereotype that the boys grew up with. Their father did not spend time with them because he re-married within two months of his divorce from Julie. In fact, the new wife had a little girl from a previous relationship. Together they had two more children. Julie's boys felt completely abandoned and rejected by their father because he left them for another family.

The boys are creating the same pattern of abandonment in their respective relationships.

Other Forms of Abandonment:
Many kids are given up for adoption each year. This fact creates abandonment issues. Even if a child has not been told of the adoption, he/she may experience deep-seated abandonment issues. Children often do not understand the reasons behind the need for adoption.

Children often intuit what Mom and Dad are thinking and feeling while they are in Mom's womb. Children know if Mom is thinking of relinquishing parental rights. While in the womb, the little souls may erroneously believe they can fix conditions that are compromising to their health and emotional balance.

It is a sad commentary that in everyday life so many children have been abused, abandoned, or neglected mentally, physically, and emotionally. Many forms of abandonment are connected to these abuses.

Have you suffered abuse or abandonment in your past? If so, it is time to let go of that story. Let's write a new chapter in your life. This takes time, effort, and much work.

Many children endure parents who possess multiple addictions. Whether the issue involves drugs, alcohol, relationships, or being a workaholic, children of addictive parents have a high probability of following in the same addictive path as their parents. Of course, they can make a decision to take a more enlightened journey.

Negative patterns, beliefs and behaviors are learned and can be altered to suit a healthier life style. Some of these patterns keep you blocked. If you take the time to clean up your past, then you can focus on creating the future you desire.

My Victim Pattern:

In 1987, I became extremely ill. I was put in the hospital for ulcerative colitis. I was left there to die. The doctors had informed me that my colon was too far gone and they could not even remove it.

After several days of prayers and pleading, I knew I would live. After several weeks, I was released from the hospital. I was determined to discover my spiritual path. God had rescued and saved me yet another time. Why? I know that I had asked to be saved, but God did not have to answer my prayer. I wanted more answers and information. I wanted to gain a greater understand of God and how prayers could change future areas of health and spiritual welfare.

This meant that I wanted to determine why God served mankind. I wanted to unmask the wholeness of the universe. Many religions teach that God dwells outside of us not within. I believe the later part to be true. I wanted to study multiple philosophies to see if I could find something that resonated with my spiritual perspective. I also wanted to gain a greater understanding about the intrinsic nature of the Universe.

When I got home from the hospital, I immediately went to the bookstore. Looking for answers to my question, I began reading different metaphysical texts and self-help books. I had moved beyond my limitations of religious beliefs to a greater understanding of God.

Now I no longer bought into some of my religious beliefs as I had done in the past. I decided to focus on other philosophies to find what they believed to be true about God. The churches I had attended always preached about a judgmental God. In addition, many pastors mentioned that if you performed evil actions, you would go to hell until you took God as your savior and confessed all your sins.

I had learned many negative beliefs during my childhood church attendance. Experiencing the wrath of God never felt correct. I had always felt that God was a Being that loved me. I wanted to find others who held holistic beliefs similar to mine.

I read books from the following authors: Dr. Doreen Virtue, Wayne Dyer, Debbie Ford, and Dr. Brian Weiss, Dr. Deepak Chopra, and the Dalai Lama, just to name a few.

Though as a child I felt God had abandoned me many times, but now, for the first time, I felt God was standing behind me. Each day I prayed for guidance and direction to help me heal. I felt an urgency within that drove me to seek out the core issue that had initially created the ulcerative colitis. I was not sure what I was holding onto, but apparently my body was trying to tell me that something was wrong. I vowed to God that if He would let me live, I would seek out the answers and heal my body. I also agreed to serve God and to help others.

All in all, this was a very tough year for me. Six months after getting out of the hospital I ended up in surgery and had a hysterectomy. While recovering from my hysterectomy, I kept asking God and the angels to help me change all aspects my life.

For some reason, I had always felt a connection to angels. It seemed easier to trust the angels than to help me. I assumed it was because they felt more real to me than God did.

I believed God sent angels to everyone who asked for their assistance. Many times I felt the presence of angels around me. Deep within the recesses of my mind, I thought I had a memory of being able to see and talk to my angels when I was a child. I began talking to my angels again. I needed help.

"Angels, I never seem to have enough money. I failed at my prior businesses. I want to know why. I want to change my life. I want to be healthy. I need answers. Show me what to do next. I know you are there. I remember seeing you when I was little. Angels, I believe I have a guardian angel. I talked to you when I was little. You took care of me. You helped me then. Why are you not helping me now? Why am I having so many problems in my life? Just talk to me again like you used to. Help me understand all of this. Help me understand why my life is turning out the way it is."

Is This the Path?:

Three days after I asked the angels for help, a man walked up to me in a parking lot and handed me a flyer. He said, "You need to go to this workshop and should sign up right away. It's what you have been looking for."

I glanced at the flyer and looked up to ask him a question, but he was gone. I didn't understand how he could have disappeared to because we were in the middle of an empty parking lot. It was as if he had vanished into thin air.

Much later, I realized that man was an angel who had appeared in human form to make sure I would receive the help I had been seeking. The flyer detailed a workshop I felt compelled to attend. This workshop served as the beginning of my healing path.

We started the workshop by identifying our goals. I learned you have to clean up your past in order to create the future the way you desire it to be. I was not quit sure how the program was going to work considering I had no early childhood memories.

Saturday after lunch, we started clearing out past negative emotions such as anger, fear, guilt and sadness. Dr. Tad James, the facilitator, guided us to go back to the root cause the very first event of guilt. Tad guided us to go back into the past.

I let his voice guide me and I floated back to age two, the root cause of my guilt. I was looking down on the event and could see it so clearly. I was so surprised that I was able to see these memories since my conscious mind couldn't remember anything before age ten.

I was aware of me sitting on the floor playing with my dolls. My mom and older sister had gone shopping. Dad was in the same room with me watching football on the television.

During a commercial my dad said to me, "Judy, you are a bad girl."

I shook my head no. I knew I had only spoken a few words at this age, no sentences.

Dad repeated, "Judy, you are a bad girl."

I looked at him and said, "No, I'm not a bad girl."

He said, "Well, if you want to be a good girl then come here." I went over and he pulled me up onto his lap. He was sitting in a recliner chair with his legs up. He said, "If you want to be a good girl then you have to touch me here." He had unzipped his pants and you know the rest.

All of this was evolved as if I were watching a movie on T.V. I could see myself not wanting to touch Dad and yet, at the same time, feeling obliged as I wanted to be a good girl. I could see my confusion and I wished my mommy had been there so I could ask her what I should do. But Mom was not home. Dad kept pushing me to touch him. Dad took my hand and placed it on his penis and told me to rub him up and down.

He kept talking to me. He said, "If you do this for me, I will love you. You will be my good little girl." It felt so wrong to me. He kept pushing my hand up and down on him faster and faster. I felt so guilty and confused.

After Dad was done, he said, "If you ever tell anyone about this, I will put spiders up inside your "pee pee." Never tell anyone. Besides, Mommy will never believe you anyway."

Then he tried to convince me that I was the one that wanted to touch him in the first place.

"This was really your idea. If you mention anything to your mom, I will tell her that you did it and enjoyed it."

Looking down at this event from my time line, I could see how guilty I felt. I was so confused. Seeing the truth that lay at the heart of this event was traumatic and shocking. Yet, the review of the details gave me a sense of relief.

For most of my adult life, I had the same recurring dream. I saw myself as a child standing with my back against my bedroom wall holding my pillow crying and saying, "No, not tonight, please no, don't touch me, don't hurt me! Please! Please! Oh, no."

I finally understood so much. I understood why I had always been so afraid of Dad. I knew I never allowed myself be alone in the same room with him, if I could help it. But, I never knew why I acted that way. Now I knew. I got the message. Tad, guided us to release whatever guilt we discovered from our past event.

Next, Tad had us start floating back towards the present. As I was coming back to the present, I could see eight additional years of my dad sexually abusing me. He threatened to put spiders and snakes inside me so I obediently kept quiet. I was afraid. Dad had convinced me that it was my fault. I finally understood why I was afraid of the dark. Dad sexually abused me during the night in the dark with my bedroom door shut. My mom never appeared to protect me from his sexual advances.

Dad had abandoned me emotionally throughout my childhood. The only time dad was there was when he wanted me sexually. I grew up confusing sex and love. Later, I attracted men that were also emotionally unavailable.

My mom played the victim role. I followed her pattern. Mom would make many comments referring to how she had to handle the whole house and she raised us five kids by herself. Mom continually mentioned how demanding my father was.

Later, while I was married, I recognized how I always felt I had to do everything around the house. I remember telling people how I had to work full-time, raise the three kids, do all the house work, yard work, grocery shopping, laundry, and cooking. My husband did nothing other than work forty-hours a week. Woe is me. On and on I would go. I was very good at playing the victim.

My weekend with Tad James was extremely enlightening. Discovering all the abuse attached to my father, I wanted to continue to find ways to heal. I began recognizing many negative patterns I experienced with men. My dad only wanted me sexually and every man I had attracted in my adult life also only wanted me sexually. Here was a pattern that I was anxious to change.

I used Time Line Therapy® to begin healing other emotions attached to my dad. In addition to Time Line Therapy®, I also realized I needed to forgive my dad and myself for my part in the sexual abuse. Forgiving myself was most important because I could see that even at age two I thought I should have been able to stop dad. I started with the forgiveness by writing the following letter. (I never mailed the letter; it just helped me to write it.)

September 1, 1990

Dear Dad,

It was wrong of you to touch me and force me to touch you. I can forgive you because I think you must be very sick to sexually abuse your own daughters. I really don't see how a father could do such awful things to his own flesh and blood. I must assume that you have some sort of pain of your own that has caused you to be this way.

So many memories of my childhood are devastating to me. I now understand why I have had such low self-esteem and self-hatred. I can only pray that I can forgive myself for my part in this abuse.

As I write this letter trying to come from the perspective of my younger years, I can remember how afraid I was. I remember thinking that I wanted my dad to love me. You would tell me that you will if I touched you. Can you see how I ended up confusing love and sex? Dad, do you have any idea of how much emotional damage you caused in my life?

I wish you could understand that the events that transpired in my early years with you affected my life in a traumatic way. I have not been able to have a loving, trusting relationship with any man because of what you did to me.

Dad, I know you did the best you could, but honestly, I wished I had picked a different family. I always felt so abandoned by you. And now remembering my childhood brings up hate, rage, anger, sadness and grief. I think I will grieve what could have been and never was for such a long time.

Dad, I am writing this letter for my own healing. I know I need to forgive you so I can let go and move on. I am doing that with this letter. Even though you will never read this, it is helping me to tell you how I feel. The sad part for me is that you cannot own up to your part in all of this. I pray that you will someday be able to admit what you did and then forgive yourself.

I know I am supposed to love you because you are my father, but I am not ready to do that at this point. It will take time. I am growing and learning new spiritual beliefs in order to help me understand and make sense of all of this. My new knowledge is what is allowing me to forgive you. Maybe someday I can grow enough to love you.

Love,
Judy

X X X

Clearing Sadness:
During my weekend workshop with Tad James, Sunday morning it was time to clear out sadness. Floating back to the root cause of my sadness popped me into a past life. (This was strange considering I did not believe in past lives at this time.)

> *I can tell I am in Europe. I am standing near the ocean saying good-bye to a man I am in love with. (The man that I was saying goodbye to is a man that is in this workshop sitting towards the back of the room. I had seen him on break and his nametag said 'Rio'.)*
>
> *I am crying as we are saying good-bye. He does not know that I am pregnant with his baby. We are not married. He is leaving to sail on one of Christopher Columbus' ships. He promises to come back for me.*
>
> *He never comes back. I can see that he does not come back for me because he dies. I have the baby alone. I never love again. I am so sad and lonely. I am kicked out of my family for disgracing them with my unwed pregnancy.*
>
> *I realized that my mother in that life is my older sister in my current life. I now have an understanding of why I never liked my older sister this life.*

I released the sadness. While waiting for the rest of the group, I was floating out into my future looking around. I could see that Rio was going to ask me to go to lunch with him. I knew he was going to say, "So, where do you want to go?" How could I think this?

Tad brought us back to the present and we broke for lunch. The lady sitting next to me asked if we could go to lunch together. We were walking out of the room when Rio walked up to me and said.

"So, where do you want to go?"

"Oh, my gosh, I knew you were going to say that," I mumbled.

"Yes, I know."

"No, you don't get it. I knew you were going to say it exactly the way you did," I explained.

"Yes, I know."

"No, you don't get it."

"Yes, I do."

Obviously, I was the one not getting it.

The three of us went to lunch. Silence. I was too busy trying to figure out what had just happened. After lunch, Rio and I were walking back into the classroom when he whispered. "I can't be with you now. I have two little girls that need me. But I will always love you." Then he walked over to his seat leaving me standing there with my mouth open.

I was trying so hard to figure this all out. I needed more time. I wanted to talk to Rio alone and ask him what all this meant. But, Tad was telling everyone to sit down so we could get started. I couldn't ask Rio anything.

At the end of the day, I was signing my name to a mailing list when Rio leaned over towards me and said, "So, your name is Judy this life. I like that."

I turned to face him and he was gone. Lost in the crowd of two hundred fifty people, I could not find him. I was frantic. I had to talk to him. Where is he?

I went home confused. What was this whole thing really about? I could tell I loved this man even though I did not know him.

I could not sleep. I could not concentrate. I felt so strange. I even got a migraine because I was so upset. I felt like I was in his truck riding to Amarillo with him. I did not even know if he was driving a truck. But it felt like a truck. I felt like we were talking like old friends.

I got up the next morning without having slept. I still felt so connected to Rio and could not seem to let him go. I went back to the hotel where the workshop was held hoping someone could help me. I knew they were still there doing a special "Huna" day. However, I did not have the money to sign up for this extra day to learn about Hawaiian Spiritualism.

Reaching the hotel, I found Darlene, who worked with Tad. She assisted me. I explained to her how I felt I was still connected to Rio. I felt disassociated and not attached to my body. I could not seem to get him out of my mind. Could she help me?

Darlene said, "You have a cord connecting you to Rio. It is called an "AKA" cord. It is silvery white." She showed me how to pull the cord out of my body. This stopped the energy flow between us.

On one hand, I was very sad to pull the cord. On the other hand, I felt relieved to get back to normal. Rio and I had such a strong connection from that past life that we reconnected that cord when we met.

To this day, I wonder about my time with Rio. I hope for an opportunity to meet him again and ask about that day. Did he know I was in the truck with him? What else did he experience? How did he know that I knew he was going to ask me to lunch? I had so many unanswered questions.

My experiences at this workshop were very profound. I knew I needed to keep healing. Forgiving Dad was the first thing on my list.

X X X

I went to Hawaii to further study with Dr. Tad James so that I could identify more patterns from my childhood and begin to release and heal them. Identifying beliefs and patterns that keep us stuck is a great step in manifesting your soul's spiritual journey.

Next, you will want to determine what you came to earth to learn.

Chapter 3

Probable Lessons

"Be not the slave of your own past. Plunge into the sublime seas, dive deep and swim far, so you shall come back with self-respect, with new power, with an advanced experience that shall explain and overlook the old."

Ralph Waldo Emerson

There are many probable lessons that we come to Mother Earth to learn. Many of us are learning lessons connected to love, trust, and forgiveness. How we choose to learn these lessons is based on free will. In addition, there are many other lessons to learn in life besides these three that we will discuss in this chapter.

Love:

"Love created me like Itself," according to *A Course in Miracles*. The premise is that "If Love created you like Itself; this Self must be in you. And somewhere in your mind it is there for you to find." [1]

A Course in Miracles also states "Love holds no grievances." To hold a grievance is to forget who you are. Forgetting who you are is seeing yourself as a body instead of the spiritual being in a human body. [2]

When you forget who you are, you forget you are Love. Your ego seems to split you off from Source. "For he who holds grievances denies he was created by Love, and his Creator has become fearful to him in his dream of hate," as stated in *A Course in Miracles*.[3]

There are many ways to work on the lesson of love. Perhaps you start with remembering where you came from and learn about love of self and next love of others. Loving yourself unconditionally is one of the most difficult lessons to learn. Out of my clients, less than 5 percent actually say they love themselves unconditionally.

Many clients tell me that they don't feel they are good enough to be able to love themselves. Many of these clients have related that they could never remember a time when they did love themselves. They could not seem to remember a single event in their childhood that gave them a sense of positive self-regard.

Leslie, one of my clients, had a belief that she did not deserve to be loved by anyone. She continually created situations that were self-punishing and self-sabotaging. She never seemed to attract positive men to her who would treat her with respect. She believed that she was not pretty enough to lure a good-looking, nice man. She truly believed she was ugly and did not deserve to be loved.

Consequently, she never attracted love into her life. Leslie did attract men that abused her sexually and verbally. Her latest boyfriend reminded her daily about how ugly she was. He put forth the notion that she was lucky to have him around because nobody else would want her.

Are you settling for something less than perfect in your life? Are you continually attracting negative partners? Do you feel that you somehow have missed the boat on love and that it is too late? Look inside at your beliefs about love.

As a grandma, I listen to my 8-year old granddaughter, Gracie, frequently saying things about herself: "I'm no good, I'm stupid, I don't deserve to have anything because I make so many mistakes." I realize most people begin as children saying negative things to themselves. How could Gracie possibly love herself with this sort of negative self-talk going on?

Many of you spend a lot of time judging yourself as well as others. When you stand in judgment of yourself and others you are operating from your head, intellect, and your ego; not your heart. Drop down into your heart and see if there is any reason not to love yourself.

When you stand in your head, intellect, or ego, you are coming from a place in which a lot of negative issues are being expressed. Specifically, the ego is the source of fear, anger, hate, doubts. In contrast, when you are truly coming from your heart, you show great compassion and reflect unconditional love.

God created you in His image. Therefore, what is there about you NOT to love? When you are focusing on the negative; that is what you see. Spend time focusing on the good things about yourself. Heal and forgive yourself.

Is your love unconditional? Does it come with various sets of conditions? Many parents love their kids conditionally. For example, I will only love you: **if** you keep your room clean, **if** you get good grades, **if** you do well in sports, **if** you do exactly as I say.

Unconditional love is what you feel and express towards animals and newborn babies. You just love them, period. Right? They do not have to earn that love. Love evolves in a natural way.

Trust:

Trust serves as both an emotional and logical act. Emotionally, it is the way you expose your vulnerability to people, but believe they will not take advantage of your openness. Logically, it is where you have assessed the probabilities of gain and loss and concluded that the person in question will behave in a predictable manner.

According to David Straker of Changing Minds he defines trust as the following:

Definition 1: "Trust means being able to predict what other people will do and what situations will occur. If we can surround ourselves with people we trust, then we can create a safe present and an even better future.

Definition 2: Trust means making an exchange with someone when you do not have full knowledge about them, their intent and the things they are offering to you.

Definition 3: Trust means giving something now with an expectation that it will be repaid, possibly in some unspecified way at some unspecified time in the future.

Definition 4: Trust means enabling other people to take advantage of your vulnerabilities—but expecting that they will not do this. " [4]

The above definition of trust is connected to other people. But, what about trusting in you? Trusting in yourself means going inward to your intuition. Shakti Gawain says it nicely,

"Trusting your intuition means tuning in as deeply as you can to the energy you feel, following that energy moment to moment, trusting that it will lead you where you want to go and bring you everything you desire. It means being yourself, being real and authentic in your communications, being willing to try new things because they feel right, doing what turns you on." [5]

We are all born with intuition. Your intuition is that gut feeling or knowingness that you experience deep within your self. I have heard many people say that they do not trust their intuition. Realize, your intuition is the inner voice of God. It exists separate from that voice from your ego self. Trust that your intuition is never wrong.

Shakti Gawain also says, "Every time you don't follow your inner guidance, you feel a loss of energy, a loss of power, a sense of spiritual deadness." [6]

Trusting your intuition means you are in the habit of trusting God and have a well-defined sense of self. Many people go through life making choices that turn out badly. Because of this propensity, they stop trusting their inner guidance. Specifically, they do not realize that those particular choices are probably made based on old patterns, rather than intuitive inspiration.

I've heard people say, "Oh, if I had just followed my gut, I would not be in the mess I am in now." True intuition guides you towards positive things. Unfortunately, your ego is wrong on most occasions. Your ego is not the logical part of your brain; here it is the fear and doubt part that you are using. Have you ever had a feeling that you knew you should do something about, but you didn't trust your feelings enough to follow through? Trust is a big thing. Release the limiting decision to not trust yourself or your gut feelings.

If you can't trust yourself, then whom can you trust? If you don't trust yourself, find out why. Go back into your past to the root cause, the first time you made the decision to not trust yourself. What was going on? What other emotions are attached to that specific decision?

Then follow the steps previously detailed (see the summary in Chapter 7), the way in which you can eliminate those feelings from your body. Replace those old feelings with new feelings of trust.

One of my clients, Sarah, told me she couldn't trust herself because she always made poor decisions. "Why do you have to think so black and white, Sarah? Why not think of it as just a lesson you are learning and that it took those circumstances for you to learn the lesson." I asked.

Sarah is judging herself because she feels she has made poor decisions. She does not look to the root cause behind her decision making. What was the motivation behind the decision? What are the patterns or lessons that are pertinent to the situation?

For example, say you are buying a new house. You are wondering if it is a good investment or not. Go inside your heart and see if the purchase is for your highest good. Do not look at choices as either good or bad. Clearly, we make what seems to be the best choice for us at the time that we make it. Try to re-evaluate and reassess the issues behind your decision making. What is motivating you or guiding you to choose some things over others?

Ignoring Your Gut:

During the course of your life, how many times have you had a gut feeling about a person, yet you chose to ignore that gut feeling? For example, my client Sue had a feeling the first time she met Tom (now her ex-husband) that there would be lots of problems. Sue had a feeling that she should immediately walk away. She ignored her gut feeling. She wanted a relationship no matter what. Her ego told her that she could fix him.

Does that mean she made a bad choice? Yes, because she ignored her intuitive guidance. Many of you have had relationships that you took on even though you sensed future difficulties. Why? Perhaps Sue was still running the same old patterns. Until she finally learned her lesson, she continued making choices based on old patterns. She made the best choice for her at the time of the decision based on the information she had. Despite their obvious differences, Tom helped Sue to learn a lot. Had she made a different choice, she might not have learned all those poignant life lessons.

Throughout our work together, Sue realized that she and Tom came together to work out their karmic debts. Karmic debts consist of unfinished lessons from prior lives. In one past life, it was clear to Sue that they had been married. Tom was very controlling and jealous. Sue was very submissive. Moreover, in that particular life, despite the fact that Sue was very unhappy, she stayed with Tom until death.

In this present life, when Sue realized the marriage would fail, she walked away. The past karmic debt was now complete. The lesson had to do with Sue feeling deserving of love and happiness. During her past life with Tom, Sue noticed that she had stayed married despite her unhappiness. In that lifetime when Sue passed away she was still very angry at having wasted her life in a loveless marriage. In her current life, Sue was able to walk away so she could find love and happiness somewhere else.

Today, Sue is grateful that she has learned to trust her intuitive self. It is always the ego that creates the doubts and causes us to second-guess our intuition. (Chapter 7 will teach you how to shrink your ego so that you can follow your inner guidance.)

It is really important to begin to look at the choices you are making and discover why you are making those choices. Start paying attention to the self-talk inside your head. Your self-talk speaks volumes about what is going on inside of you. Pay attention. Then use that as a guide to the patterns and beliefs that need to be changed and healed.

Nancy's Belief:

Another client, Nancy, finds that she rarely trusts other people. Nancy believes that everyone is out to get her. That is indicative of the fact that she does not trust herself. If you do not trust yourself, how can you possibly trust anyone else?

Nancy does not trust herself because of the sexually abusive childhood she experienced. She grew up knowing that she could never trust her parents. Life never seemed safe for her. Accordingly, she developed the belief that she could not trust anyone around her. This belief has kept Nancy isolated from others. Start noticing how your lack of trust can affect other areas of your life. Attempt to move towards changing those old beliefs and outdated dysfunctional patterns.

As you start trusting yourself, you can subsequently observe your thoughts and change the negative thoughts to positive ones. Your inner guidance brings direction to your life. Learning how to have positive self-talk will also support your self-trust.

Understand that your ego wants to keep you separated from

God. The ego contains every negative thought you have ever experienced. For example, you can hear your parents and other negative people echo inside your head. If you took the voice inside your head of your mother and changed it to one that sounds like Mickey Mouse, it would not have the same effect on you that the disapproving negative voice of your mom might currently have.

Your thoughts are just thoughts. All in all, you do not need to give them any power or value. What is suggested here is to recognize the thoughts and find the emotions attached to them. Then begin to heal the emotions. The more you move towards a positive space in your life, the easier it will be to trust yourself and your inner guidance. (You can also follow the instructions in Chapter 7 to remove people from your head.)

Forgiveness:
One of the lessons many people came to earth to experience is forgiveness. This was an extremely painful lesson for Virginia to learn. Virginia picked a father that sexually abused her as a child. She sought me out for help as she was having a hard time forgiving him. I suggested a session involving past life regression to see what other life times she might have experienced with her father. (I already knew that she had a past life of abuse with her current dad. I knew she would gain some insight into her current life by re-visiting that particular past life she had with her dad.)

I put Virginia into a hypnotic state and directed her into a past life that was connected to her current father. She easily found the lifetime we were looking for. I had her view that past life as if she were watching it on T.V.

Viewing a negative situation from a disassociated position keeps you from experiencing the feelings. A dissociated position is when you are looking at a picture of you, but not looking through your own eyes. This position is less traumatic for the person.

Probable Lessons

Usually, in past life regressions, I slide the client down inside their body so they are seeing from their eyes, feeling from their bodies. This is known as an associated position.

In this particular scenario, Virginia saw she was a girl and had the exact same parents as she does in her current incarnation. In that life, however, her parents were old and her mom was bedridden. Her dad cut her hair off and made her dress like a boy so that men would not bother her. By day, Virginia tended to the sheep. At night, her mom made her have sex with her dad so Mom did not have to.

In that specific past life, her mom died when she was about twelve. Life had been difficult; she had been very unhappy. Virginia had no friends. Dad died when she was sixteen. All the sheep were stolen. Angry and alone, Virginia was unsure what to do for money. Feeling desperate, she went into the nearby town and obtained a job as a prostitute in the local tavern.

Virginia died in her thirties filled with anger, hate, and rage. Truly, Virginia hated her parents and the life they forced her to live. Hate, bitterness, and blame had become a way of life.

After reviewing this past life and its disappointments, Virginia found she created a similar scenario in this life. In her current life, she has the same parents and experienced sexual abuse in her childhood. Creating the same experience in her current life gave her the opportunity to learn forgiveness. If she had chosen to hold onto her anger, she would have empowered her dad and never experienced forgiveness. Instead, forgiveness gave her back her power.

The "forgiveness method" I taught Virginia is outlined in Chapter 7. Virginia forgave herself for not trusting in herself. She forgave herself for her part in her childhood sexual abuse. She forgave her dad for sexually abusing her. She forgave her mom for not protecting her from her dad's exploitive behavior. Forgiving her mom was the hardest thing for her to do. Virginia knew that her mom knew Dad was abusing her. Her mom did nothing to stop it. That seemed devastating to Virginia.

Virginia believes her mom chooses to live in denial in her current life, because she did not have the resources to deal with the situation. Had her mom confronted her dad and asked him to leave, then her mom would have to support all five children on her own. Virginia's mom did not work and; therefore, could not face that possibility. Denial served to operate better for her mom's survival.

Parents and Children:

We pick our parents and then later our children to help us work out our life lessons. Such lessons may contain unfinished business from past lives or simply new lessons for the current life journey. Usually, the most difficult lessons will occur among family members. What is your most difficult lesson?

One client, Elaine, said her most difficult lesson as a mother was recognizing that she was controlling. When I explained to Elaine how patterns and behaviors are created from childhood wounds, she suddenly understood why she had developed into a controlling and domineering adult. For some reason, she thought she was only controlling in her personal sphere of love relationships. Strangely enough, she failed to see that she was a controlling mother to her children; a pattern that persisted into their adult lives.

Discovering Patterns:

As I was teaching Nancy, another client, how to discover patterns, she began to determine negative patterns that operated in her life as well. Nancy's son, Jason, paired off with Shannon and had a baby out of wedlock. That relationship ended in battle. Then, Jason married Heather. Now, he had two extremely controlling women in his life. Jason seemed to be in constant conflict with both of them. Upon further examination, Nancy realized that the controlling pattern originated from her. In fact,

Jason's father rarely played a role in his life. Therefore, Nancy could see that Jason attracted women to him that mirrored the wounds from his early childhood years.

Nancy had to search to determine see where and how those wounds occurred. She realized that she was very rigid regarding her need to have a clean house. Nancy was an organized person; Jason was sloppy. Nancy wanted his room picked up and cleaned weekly. When Jason did not clean the room the way Nancy wanted it, they would argue and bicker. Nancy would put every-thing left on the floor in a trash bag and throw it out for the trash man. Jason would bring the bag back in and scatter it all over his room again. Nancy would ground him. Nancy could now see how that created a negative pattern that was in need of being healed.

Once Nancy opened herself to the idea that she seemed to be a controlling mother, it was easy for her to see all the ways she still tried to control Jason as an adult. Since, she had always felt that she was a loving and caring mom; it was difficult for Nancy to admit that she was overly controlling. Somehow being controlling sounded as if she were an unloving mother. Later, Nancy realized that being controlling is a behavior that in itself does not reflect or demonstrate a lack of love.

Eventually, Nancy discovered another lesson through examining the drama/trauma in Jason's life. Nancy was carrying Jason and all his problems inside her physical body. Each time Jason called to tell his mom what drama was going on in his life, Nancy could feel the way in which she continued to add more emotional baggage to her own pre-existing issues that lived within her body.

She used the "roll-up" method detailed in Chapter 7, to roll Jason and all the emotions up out of her body. After this process was complete, Nancy couldn't believe how much lighter she felt. The lesson here meant she needed to understand that carrying her son's baggage did not serve either individual. Instead, it weighed them both down.

Nancy could help Jason better by teaching him how to roll all those emotions up out of his body. Nancy needed to stop trying to control the outcomes in Jason's life. In fact, Nancy would serve Jason better by holding the intent of a positive outcome.

Even after pregnancy a mother can "carry" her child's emotional problems in any part of her body including heart, belly, and legs. Are you emotionally carrying someone in your body? It does not have to be a child. For example, you can carry a spouse, parent, or friend. You do not want to carry anyone emotionally. To remedy the situation, follow the steps in Chapter 7 to roll that person and the emotional baggage up and out of your body.

Chapter 4

Taking Responsibility

*"Responsibility is the thing people dread most of all. Yet, it is
the one thing in the world that develops us, gives us manhood
or womanhood fiber."*
Frank H. Crane

You have discovered how beliefs, patterns, and behaviors are
formed. You have also learned what some of your probable
lessons in life might be. Now, it is time to look at how to take
responsibility for the outcomes in your life, both positive and
negative.

Your Responsibility:
You manifest and create everything that happens to you, both
good and bad, based on what you choose to experience and the
self-talk that goes on in your head. If you would learn to accept
responsibility for your thoughts and actions, then you would
regain your personal power. Thus, taking responsibility would
allow you to move towards healing.

When you ignore your thoughts, you stay blocked. What you
resist continues to persist for a reason. When you blame life,
God, or others for the negative events that have happened in
your life, then you are not assuming responsibility for your life.
Instead, you are playing the victim. This assists you in giving
your power away. Instead, when you take responsibility for your
life, you are accessing your personal source of power.

Taking responsibility means addressing your thoughts. Start
by noticing the self-talk in your head. Every time you say
negative things to yourself, you would want to stop and replace

it with positive self-talk. This will take time to retrain yourself; however, you can do it.

One negative thought is enough to poison the impact of positive thoughts. It is as if you are taking one step forward and two steps back. You never seemed to get anywhere. When you began to understand negative thoughts are enough to hold you back, then, you can begin to change them. You want to stay positive.

The following analogy taught me how one negative thought can poison good thoughts. Take a glass of soda, use it to represent your negative thoughts. Take a glass of water; let it represent your positive thoughts. Now, put a couple of spoonfuls of water, positive thoughts, into your soda containing negative thoughts. Nothing really changes, does it? So, your positive thoughts don't override the negative thoughts. But, if you put one spoon of negative thought (soda) into your water, it completely poisons your positive container. This example shows you how negative thoughts have such a negative impact on your life.

Truly, you want to stay focused on positive thoughts. How do you accomplish this? The following details the way in which you can address this.

The first step involves turning down the volume of the voice inside your head. The voice represents your ego and all the old scripts from your past. This particular voice is the one that is speaking to you that evokes all the negative reactions.

In addition, you would want to use the self-talk to help you get started in your healing process. What are you saying to yourself and why? Go back the first time you ever began saying those negative things to yourself. Look at the patterns and find the origins for them. Heal the wounds associated to the negative talk. Then change the self-talk.

Issac Newton used the principle of cause and effect as the basis of his law of thermodynamics: He stated that every action has an equal and opposite reaction. Cause and effect applies to everything, including your thoughts.

Many times you blame others for your circumstances instead of taking responsibility for what happens in your life. When you run this pattern, you are coming from effect. When you are willing to take responsibility, you have the power to change your circumstances. When initiating this pattern, you are coming from cause.

Instead of blaming others for your circumstances, look to see why and how you created certain situations in your life. Blaming is a victim pattern. Tell yourself that you will no longer play the victim role. Take back your power.

Many of your self-punishing patterns and self-destructive behaviors are created by your ego in order to prevent you from connecting to God. Many of you create so many busy distractions in your life that you could not possibly listen to your inner guidance. Your ego is the problem as it can well understand its separation from God. When you stop listening to your ego and start connecting into your heart, your life will begin to make sense.

Assuming responsibility for your life should be done without judgment and guilt. Love yourself is the rule here. If you judge yourself about the things you have created in your life, then you are not honoring your process. Neither are you coming from a space of love. Healing is a process that involves many facets of self-understanding.

As humans, many of you are very stubborn and learn things the hard way. The good side to this is that when you do learn your lessons, you have it and will not have to repeat old debilitative patterns.

Past Life Issues:

Some of your issues come from past life events. A prime example of that is the experience of one of my clients. Ted was in a wheelchair and I talked him into letting me do a past life regression on him. I thought it would be very healing for him to see why he had landed in a wheelchair.

Even though Ted had been in a car accident when he was a teenage, I could see the source of his paralysis lay in the form of a karmic debt from a past life event. In other words, I believe there is a reason for every condition we endure. I knew the car accident had a purpose in Ted's life. I could see that his decision to be in a wheelchair this life time stemmed from an event in one of his past lives.

I did not tell Ted what I saw; I simply wrote it down so we could compare notes after his regression. This allowed Ted to see for himself the reason connected to his accident. I knew this information would help him to release and to heal his anger.

Ted was an easy subject. He went into trance quickly. He immediately went to a lifetime where he was involved in a chariot race. Ted wanted very much to win the race. He rounded a corner going too fast and ran over a lady. He kept going even though he knew he had hurt her. Ted's ego wanted so much to win the race that he did not care about her.

Later Ted learned that the lady he ran over had lost both of her legs and the use of one arm. Ted never went to apologize to her or help her in any way. He silently wondered about her over the years and carried some guilt, but in his mind he tried to convince himself that it was her fault for being too close to the track. Ted died that life carrying a lot of guilt for his actions.

Ted needed to come back and pay his karmic debt to the lady he had hurt. Through experiencing a life in a wheelchair, Ted was able to clear his karmic debt. Ted had put off the karmic debt for many lifetimes. Now, he finally agreed he would deal with it this life. Seeing this entire event helped Ted to understand why he had created the car accident. It enabled him to forgive himself for the wrong that he had caused in both lives. It helped him to release and heal all the anger he was carrying inside.

Shadow Side:

Everyone has a good and bad side. The bad or dark side of us is known as our shadow side. Having both the good and bad sides brings a balance to us.

Debbie Ford has published a wonderful book called, *The Dark Side of the Light Chasers*.[1] In her work, she states that we must go into the dark in order to bring forth the light. She further states that when you suppress any feelings, you are also suppressing their polar opposite. That means that if you deny your ugliness, you actually lessen your beauty. If you deny your fear, then you minimize your courage.

This does not mean you need to live in the dark side, but you need to recognize that you do possess a dark side. Sometimes you need the dark side so that you can experience circumstances and feelings and then move back into the light. This also gives you a contrast to gain a better understanding of the good and bad.

There are many people that spend too much time chasing the light only to eventually succumb to the more darkness. Carl Jung stated, "One does not become enlightened by imagining figures of light, but by making the darkness conscious." In other words, own and embrace your shadow. Doing so will give you the knowledge to search for what lies within you.

When you ignore the shadow side of you, it will appear anyway. Your shadow side promotes the negative aspects about you that you do not like. The shadow side is many things such as: fear, greed, and jealousy, anger, selfishness, laziness, control, and hatred just to name a few. The dark side is that part of you that lives in fear and denial as well as repression.

It is time to heal yourself and bring love back into your life. It is time to bring the light into the darkness. When you do this, you begin to find that place of peace and harmony that your soul is searching for.

Internal Conflict:

Many people possess both inner and outer conflict. In fact, I had such a client recently. Mary presents as a happy-go-lucky person on the outside, but on the inside, I could see her deep sadness, sorrow, and depression. Her inner self was not balanced with her outer self. Mary was not consciously aware of the inner conflict. Having a conflict such as this keeps you in limbo. Once Mary could see that if she healed her sadness, sorrow and depression, then she could become the happy go lucky person she presented to the world. Hiding her inner feelings was telling herself a lie. These unresolved emotions inside Mary were beginning to manifest as illness in her body. Is your inner and outer self out of balance?

The internal conflict also shows up when saying things to others that you really do not feel or mean. You might be telling people that you have money or are creating money, but inside you do not feel worthy of having money. This conflict has to be resolved or you will not have any money.

For people that want a relationship, your outer world needs to mirror your inner desire for a relationship. One such client that told me she was desperate to have a permanent relationship leading to marriage. Because we were friends, I often visited her house and noticed that her house did not reflect her desire to have a man.

I noticed her master bedroom closets were filled with so many clothes leaving no room for a man's clothes. The drawers were all filled to the brim. She even had pictures on the walls of single women. I explained to her that she needed to make room in the bedroom for a man. I told her to empty part of the closet and a couple of the drawers. Take those pictures of single women down and put up pictures of couples. Her outer world had to match her inner desires.

She made all the changes I suggested and in less than a month she met a wonderful man. They married a year later. That was a few years ago and they are still very happy. She took responsibility for the reality she had been creating and changed it so that she could have what she wanted.

Overweight Issues:

Our country has become an obese nation. I hear people say that they have tried every diet out there and they still can't seem to loose any weight. Many people eat emotionally putting on weight trying to push the emotional issues aside.

The kinesthetic people (touchy/feelers) of the world have a tendency to put on more weight than the visual or auditory people. That is because those of you who are touchy feelers take on other people's emotions and internalize them. After a while, carrying other people's feelings, along with your own issues, becomes too heavy. You substitute food for the issue and put on weight to push the feelings out and away from you. If you would stop owning other people's problems, then you would not have the need to push all those negative emotions out from your body. Therefore, you would not have the need to put on weight.

Since many overweight people have recognized that they eat emotionally, it is time to start paying attention to what you are feeling and why you are feeling it. When you can recognize what you are feeling, then you can clear those emotional issues with the techniques in Chapter 8.

In addition, the techniques in Chapter 8 will teach you how to clear other people's emotions out of your body and head. The techniques also teach you how to keep from taking on other people's emotions and problems. Learning to set boundaries with other people is an important lesson for us to learn. Setting boundaries does not mean that you do not love others; it just means that it is not useful for you to carry your family or friends' problems.

Excess weight can also serve as a protection against perceived dangers. What do you need protection from? If you have struggled with weight problems, then you have probably tried many different diets. Therefore, you already know how to lose weight better than anyone.

Paul McKenna states in his book, *I Can Make You Thin* [2] that diets do not work. McKenna's book is a must read for anyone that has suffered with weight issues. He actually teaches you NLP (Neur-Linguestic Programming) techniques that change the patterns in your brain. Following McKenna's guidance, you can eat whatever you want. He specifically details psychological techniques that re-pattern your thoughts, attitudes, and beliefs about food, your body, and yourself.

Doreen Virtue states in her book, *Constant Craving*, that it is time to heal your appetite; not kill it. Doreen states, "Overwhelming food cravings are the culprit behind every obese body, every broken diet, and every dietary related disease." [3]

Are you overweight? Is it because of emotionally based cravings? Do you believe that you just put on weight as you get older and there is nothing you can do about it? Have you put on weight to keep men away from you? Are you holding onto anger towards your parents that you have stored in your body? It is time to discover your reasons for being overweight. It is time to stop making excuses and start being proactive about changing your life. If you are unhappy with your body weight, then now is the time to truly change it.

When you truly love yourself, you take care of your body. That means you eat healthy, exercise regularly, and get enough rest.

In making these changes you want to focus on what you want, not what you don't want. If you focus on, 'I just want to lose 20 pounds,' than you will put on 20 pounds because the 20 pounds is what your focus is on. Instead, focus on 'I weigh 120 pounds,' or whatever weight you want to weigh.

Focusing on what you want is the number one key to obtaining any goal. It is known as "The Law of Attraction." It is important to watch your thoughts. Are you thinking about what you want or about what you don't want? There is a big difference.

I have a prime example of how the "law of attraction" works. Two years ago, I decided to buy a new car. After a few hours of searching, I quickly came to the conclusion that I wanted a Nissan Altima. I sat down and wrote a list of all the things I wanted in my new Altima. However, when I got to the color, I didn't know what color I wanted, I just knew I did not want red. My last two cars had been red. After writing my list, I sat and visualized me in my new car. I could feel the excitement of having everything I wanted. But again, my thoughts went to 'I don't care what color, but no red.'

Well, of course, you can guess what the color of Nissan is in my garage. It's red! Every time I open the garage door I am reminded of how I got what I put my thoughts into. Your brain does not do 'don't, or no's.' You send out the vibe of what you are thinking and that is what you get. In my case, I put energy into no red and of course I got red.

Secondary Gain:

You have learned how you should take responsibility for your thoughts and actions. In order to continue learning how to take responsibility for your life you may want to consider secondary gains. A secondary gain is something you have to gain from an illness or injury.

If you are looking at yourself and an illness or injury that you have created, please look at these issues with love and under-standing. And yes, I did say an illness you created. Again, we create everything in our lives, both good and bad.

For example, my client, Angela, called stating her husband, Mike, had hurt his back. She wanted me to see him to explain to him why he got hurt so he could heal it. She did mention that he had gone to the doctor and the doctor put him on a muscle relaxant.

When Mike arrived, I asked him what was going on in his head prior to his back injury.

He laughed and said, "Why can't a backache just be a backache?"

I replied, "Not when you know me and your wife knows that I believe there is a reason for everything." I further said, "You created the backache for a reason, so tell me, what is going on inside you?"

That made him angry because he thought I was blaming him. "It is not about blame. It is about taking responsibility," I explained to him.

"Mike, come and sit in my office and let me help you look at why you created the backache."

Once he could see what had occurred, he could find a way to release the pain. He could let go of the pain. I know that might sound a little harsh if this is new to you, but keep going because it is really empowering.

"Mike, what kind of the self-talk was going on in your head for the last couple of days prior to the back injury?

He was lifting a boat motor and just assumed that it was too heavy and that he strained his back causing the pain. I knew there was a deeper meaning.

After some soul searching, Mike finally admitted. "I did not want to finish our basement. I had been thinking about how I could get out of doing the work. I'm not quite sure about how to finish the laundry room and enclose the furnace."

His wife, Angela, had been pushing him to finish the basement before summer arrived.

So in Mike's case, he had something to gain by having a backache. This is called a secondary gain. The injury occurred because he was feeling insecure about his ability to finish the basement. Frankly, he did not want to communicate that to Angela. In his mind, he was thinking about how he could get out of finishing the basement. His unconscious mind (which is an obedient three-year old you) says, "You want to get out of finishing the basement? I can do that for you." And, boom the low back pain came into place.

Mike did not consciously say, "How can I hurt myself to get out of finishing the basement." But, your unconscious mind brings to you that which you are thinking about. By taking responsibility of his thoughts, Mike could have avoided the back pain.

Can you see how what you are thinking is what you end up creating in your life? I was not blaming Mike for creating the backache, I was showing him how his thoughts created his injury. This is not about blame. It is about taking responsibility and therefore, gaining back your power.

If you focus your thoughts and feelings on what you want instead of what you do NOT want, can you imagine how good your life can be? In Mike's case, his thoughts went to what he did not want. Mike ended up finishing the basement with the help of a friend and Angela said he did a really nice job.

Mike has unconsciously created many illnesses in his life for attention and to get out of something. This was a pattern for him. Mike unconsciously learned this pattern from his mother who also frequently creates illness to get out of doing something she does not want to do. Helping him see this pattern put Mike in a place of choice for his future. He could acknowledge and own the pattern then release it and visualize a new way of handling situations that would be more useful to him if he wanted.

Soul Fragments:
Since my work with clients involves many different issues, I studied and learned how to help people that have had childhood abuse and trauma. Many people that are abused in early childhood are unable to cope with the trauma of abuse. Therefore, their soul fragments or splits apart from the whole being. In some cases, the actual soul fragments and then literally

leaves the body because it cannot cope with the abuse. However, in most cases, the soul just fragments.

Over the years, I have had numerous clients that were abused as a child. Since like attracts like, it was easy for me to see why I attracted these clients. Because I was able to heal from my past, the universe sends me clients so that I can assist them in their healing.

I first noticed soul fragments with my own sister and was able to assist her in integrating these soul fragments. Since that time, I have dealt with numerous clients that have had anywhere from one fragment to thirty-nine. None of them have had as many fragments as my sister. I literally can see the fragments whether they are fragmented inside the body or completely separated and attached outside of the body.

I am amazed at what kinds of different traumas people have had to go through and how their soul chooses to cope. Soul fragments are created out of fear and as a way of protecting the whole being. As a child, one does not have the resources to know how to handle such trauma. Accordingly, a part of the soul breaks off from the whole, thinking it is protecting the rest of the whole.

Even though breaking apart from the whole does not protect the being, the inability to know this is not recognized by someone so young. I have been able to pull the negative emotions and then integrate the fragments back into the whole being.

This can be a fairly easy process if there is only one split and little trauma. The more traumas and more splits the more compli- cated. Not everyone that had abuse in their childhood experi- ences fragments, however, many do. When talking with these clients most of them admitted that they knew they had different parts of themselves running the show at different times. They did not know what to do about it and were afraid to tell anyone for fear of what would happen to them.

For others, they knew they had different fragments, but they assumed it was normal and that everyone had different parts running the show at different times. Following are a few cases for you to see if you can identify with their experiences.

Diane:

In the early nineties my sister, Diane, came to Plano, Texas to stay with me for a period. She wanted me to assist in healing her. She had been diagnosed with multiple Personality Disorder by a psychiatrist. She had fragmented into 213 multiple split personalities. My gift of being intuitive helped me to see these different splits.

I worked with Diane everyday for a long time integrating her fragments. Then, we began pulling the patterns that were created from her abusive childhood. Diane and I were both sexually abused by our dad when we were little. But for whatever reason, Diane did not cope with the abuse in the same way I did. I did not split off; but Diane had fragmented into so many splits.

Diane recognized that she had many different fragments. To her, they were younger ages of herself with different aspects. Some of her fragments were boys and some were girls. Her soul fragmented these parts as a way to cope and protect the bigger whole. She had parts that would run the show at different times. All of Diane's fragments were still inside her body. It was like they would line up on a stage for me to see them.

It was interesting watching which soul fragments would take charge and what circumstances would create the take over. Diane, the sister I grew up with, was usually quiet, insecure and gentle. When one of the stronger fragments took over, she became stubborn, outspoken and displayed a hardness. One of her fragments drank and smoked. Another one cursed and carried on like a wild woman.

When one of the male fragments was dominating, she cut her hair off, threw out her purse, and bought a wallet that she carried in her back pocket just like a man. That particular fragment was very strong and stubborn. This personality aspect was very difficult and could be verbally abusive.

When we got all the fragments integrated and Diane had done all the healing she wanted to do, she decided to return to Denver. Diane had only been in Texas for three months and there was still a lot of emotional work that needed to be done. Meanwhile, though, Diane was adamant about returning home.

She sold her house in the mountains and moved in with Mom and Dad. Not such a good idea being in the same house with Dad. In fact, she still had some more healing to do. After three-failed marriages, she had lived alone for several years. Now, she just couldn't handle being alone any longer.

Diane told me, "I need to go back to my past and re-live my childhood because I do not have the memories of what happened. I need to find out for myself what really happened. I should be able to re-live my childhood by moving in with Mom and Dad and being in that same environment. And don't worry, because I know you can fix me if I split apart again."

Diane did have three fragments come back out while she lived with Mom and Dad. Eventually, she moved out of their house and into an apartment close by. Living with Dad was very difficult for Diane. Dad was verbally abusive and began to approach her sexually. Diane would tell Mom what Dad was doing; but then Dad would just convince Mom that Diane was mentally unstable.

Diane was not able to retrieve her childhood memories while living with Mom and Dad. Instead, she just became more angry and aggressive. Eventually, she joined a church and got religion. Then she decided that because the work I do was connected to hypnosis or a state of trance, it was the work of the devil. So, for now, she will continue with her three soul fragments taking turns running the show creating different personalities.

Sharon:

Sharon came to see me to work on relationship issues. She had a failed marriage and many failed relationships. She wanted to change her old patterns, heal the past, and create a relationship for her future that was loving and supportive.

I noticed on our first session that she had a soul fragment. It was a little girl about five years old that fragment outside of her body. This fragment hid behind Sharon like a frightened child. I did not mention to Sharon about her fragment at this first session. I wanted to get to know her and see if she was aware of this fragment.

One of the ways in which soul fragments are revealed is through the wording that a person uses. Sharon frequently used the phrase, "my little girl." At one of our sessions I asked her why she used that phrase.

Sharon: "I am really in touch with my little girl."

Me: "Do you have a sense of how old your little girl is?"

Sharon: "Why, yes, she is five."

Sharon's stepfather had first sexually abused her at age five. I could see that a part of her fragmented off from the whole being at that age out of fear. I asked her other questions about her five-year old child and discovered this.

Sharon: "I knew my five-year old was out side of my body, I just thought it was normal. "

Me: "Have you noticed that other people do not talk about their five-year old?"

Sharon: "Yes, but I just figured it's because I am more in touch with my inner child than they are."

She had revealed me times when she would go to parties and she could feel her five-year old child freaking out. She would have to leave. She said she had a hard time being out in crowds and so she would almost hibernate to keep her five-year old comfortable.

Sharon explained that she had worked with someone to help

her work through those abusive childhood years. She relayed to me that she was in a new relationship and her five-year old had begun freaking out again. Sharon did not understand why it was still coming up when she thought she had completely healed her past trauma.

Once I explained to her about her soul fragment, she was eager to integrate her five-year old. Immediately, she recognized how much more complete she felt. She no longer referred to her 'little girl.' Sharon is now able to have a normal sexual relationship. She says she can now be in crowds without being uncomfortable. Sharon says she felt so much more whole and complete. So far, her fragment has not popped back out and it has been over a year.

Andrea:

Andrea had been living back east when she fell ill and had to move home to her parent's house in Colorado. Now, she was dealing with physical health issues and a lack of money. Childhood wounds continued to bother her. She called me looking for guidance.

For the last year, I did phone readings for her. I told her what I felt was blocking her on the different issues she was working on. At that time, I taught her several techniques so that she could do her own healing work. She was very intuitive, but sometimes it was difficult for her to see everything that was blocking her from having what she wanted.

Andrea was really beginning to see that living in her parent's house was a very toxic environment for her. She constantly walked on eggshells because of her dad's anger and temper. She felt like she had to stay to protect her mother, but she really wanted to move out. She had been working really hard to clear out all the negative patterns and to create money. However, Andrea was just not manifesting the money to move out.

She had been asking God to bring to her awareness what she

still needed to heal so that she could manifest her new future. The universe answered her request, but not in the way she expected.

Now, she frantically called me for help saying that she felt she was having a breakdown. In fact, her therapist wanted to put her in the hospital. Andrea did not want to go and felt I could help her.

I scanned her and could see the problem. She had many different soul fragments; some inside and some outside of her body. Without telling her about the fragments, I began asking her questions as to what had seemingly triggered her "break."

The fragments did not just happen. They had been there since early childhood, she just was not aware of them. I had not mentioned them to her in the past because that was never part of what she was calling me for. Her readings were always connected to very specific issues that she was working on. However, during a couple of the readings I did mention to her she needed to heal the wounds from her abusive childhood and she said she would.

She had been having flashbacks of her childhood for the last few days and did not know how to cope with those memories. While she knew she had been sexually abused, she did not know any of the details. The flashbacks were pictures of all the details of the abuse and it was like she was reliving her childhood trauma all over again.

During Andrea's flashbacks, she could see parts of her at different ages break apart (as she called it). We identified nineteen different fragments at this point. She was so easy to work with because she was so in tune to herself, highly intuitive, and open to seeing and healing.

The first session we integrated all nineteen fragments. The first fragment started right after conception. Andrea decided that she should take on all of her mother's negative emotions to protect her mom. She also felt it was her duty to self-sacrifice because Jesus had done so.

Andrea had fragments from right after conception all the way up to age twenty-six. We found a few more during the second session. The fragments all had a purpose for separating. Most of the time these disassociations were to protect the other parts of her. Sometimes it was because of the physical torture she was put through during the sexual abuse. The man that abused her was her father's best friend. The things he did to her were so painful that she could not cope. She would break apart during the torture to avoid the pain.

The fragments have all been integrated; however, before I could get all the patterns pulled and the triggers disconnected some of the fragments would pop out again. Andrea mentioned to me that she would heal an emotion and notice a few days later that it was still there and she could not understand why. When you have fragments, you have to heal the emotions of the individual fragment and then integrate that fragmented piece. After that, you then heal the emotion of the whole being as well.

But, more importantly what I realized was that her soul was not attached to her any longer. Andrea split from her soul to protect her soul. Without her soul being attached to her, she did not have the ability to keep the fragments integrated because there was no whole to integrate the fragments with. So, at this point, a soul retrieval is required.

One of Andrea's life lessons is to learn how to avoid taking on other peoples' emotions and energy. Andrea started fragmenting at conception because she took on her mother's emotions and energy. She needed to experience what it was like to take on other people's emotions before she could learn how not to do it. She now recognizes that taking on her mother's pain did not keep her mom from feeling pain. It just meant that they both ended up in pain.

Andrea never told her parents about the sexual and physical abuse by her dad's best friend. As a child, she felt that if she took on all the abuse it would save her siblings from being abused. That is definitely the mentality of a child.

The techniques I use to integrate fragments are not in this book. The process is complicated and difficult to do on your own. I discussed fragmentation so that you would be aware of why it occurs and how it shows up.

If you believe you have soul fragments, then I suggest you find someone that knows how to do parts integration. Usually people that are trained at the Trainer or Master level of NLP are able to assist with the integration. Also, someone with extensive Huna Training should have the skills to assist.

Taking responsibility for your thoughts will change your life. You can even take responsibility for your fragments and integrate them creating a feeling of wholeness. Move from victim to empowerment.

Part Two
Opening To Your Higher Powers

"The only real valuable thing is intuition."
Albert Einstein

Chapter 5

Inner Guidance

"Every person is a God in embryo. Its only desire is to be born."
Deepak Chopra

Now that you have cleared up your past, you are ready to create your future. At this point, it is important to connect into your inner guidance or God connection so that you can determine what you want for your future. Doing this will allow you to live your best life.

Do you follow your inner guidance? That inner voice is the voice of God. Are you listening? Many individuals reach a point in their lives where they feel as if something is missing. Some people come to realize that even if they have the money, career, and love relationship they desire; they still feel a emptiness within.

Such an emptiness occurred for me in the early 90s. I truly felt I was in the dark of the night. I sat in a chair in the cold dark basement. With a gun in one hand and my Bible in the other hand, I cried. I felt an emptiness all the way down to the depths of my soul. Vacillating between silence and raging tears, I saw no reason to continue with life.

I felt completely abandoned by God and life itself. I took turns reading my Bible, begging God for help, and holding the gun to my head. I really could not understand why life was so riddled with pain and drudgery.

"God, why would you have created such hell on earth? I just don't understand."

No answer came.

For fourteen hours straight I sat in my green chair, mostly in the dark. How did I get to this point in my life where I no longer saw any reason to live? Through the night I prayed for help. I believed in God and angels. Where are the angels? Why was no one there to help me?

"Hello, I need help down here, God. Show me what to do. I want to trust in you, but I need a sign. Give me some sort of hope that I will make it through this dark of the night feeling."

Somewhere deep inside of me I remembered the importance of breathing. I started paying attention to my breath. I focused on my breath for a long time noticing my in and out breathing.

Awhile later, in the still of the night, my inner guidance told me to put the gun down. I could hear my guardian angel, Mary, begin to speak to me.

"Judy, you are loved. You are not alone. Trust. It is time to go outside. The sun is coming up on the horizon. You will be helped. You will be guided."

I followed Mary's advice. I went outside and sat in the early morning light. As I sat breathing in the light, I found my strength to continue on with my life. I discover that I had an inner knowingness that I would never again fall into the darkness. My inner guidance told me to keep breathing in the light of God. It was time to step into my power as a spiritual being. It was time to connect to God at a level I had never connected to before.

The darkness had passed. The emptiness was gone. I was grateful it had only been one night and not months. I continued to breathe. I was reminded of a passage in A Course in Miracles,

"Father, I come to You today to seek the peace that You alone can give. I come in silence. In the quiet of my heart, the deep recesses of my mind, I wait and listen for Your Voice. My Father, speak to me today. I come to hear Your Voice in silence and in certainty and love sure You will hear my call and answer me." [1]

Do you feel an emptiness inside of you that you just cannot quite put your finger on? Do you feel like there is more to life than just getting up and going to work to make the money to pay the bills to come home to go to bed and to get up to go to work to make the money, etc.? Do you just have this feeling inside of you that says you may have a bigger purpose in life, but you cannot seem to figure out what it is?

I believe the emptiness inside is because you are not connected to God. Many of you are disconnected from your emotional self, your physical body, and from God. You create all kinds of drama/trauma in your life to keep you so busy that it gives you the excuse to not listen to that inner guidance. Your inner guidance is trying to remind you that you are a spiritual being having a human experience.

You may have forgotten that you possess within everything you need to be whole and healthy. Instead, you keep looking outside of yourself to obtain that elusive source of fulfillment. However, when you connect with God or Source and follow your inner guidance, known as the voice of God, then your entire life flows more smoothly.

A Course in Miracles states,

"I was mistaken when I thought I lived apart from God, a separate entity that moved in isolation, unattached, and housed within a body. Now I know my life is God's, I have no other home, and I do not exist apart from Him. He has no Thoughts that are not part of me, and I have none but those which are of Him." [2]

If you do not reconnect to God, then you create a sense of dis-harmony in your life. If you do not connect to God or Source then you end up creating physical, mental, emotional, and spiritual disorders. Your life will feel like you are swimming upstream without a paddle. All the discord in your life is the universe's way of teaching you the importance of connecting to God. When you are connected to God, you feel like you are going with the flow of life instead of against the current. Doors open and life begin to harmonize. Such an experience reflects your being "in the zone."

So many angels exist among us these days to give us they opportunity to re-connect to God, heal ourselves, and the planet. The angels are here among us in order to remind us that God's love heals all wounds.

Sometimes it takes a major event or crises to get you to slow down long enough to look within. When you do slow down, you begin to notice that perhaps your life is not going the way you want it to go. Perhaps, you have begun to notice that you have wounds from your past. Now it is time to heal them. When you begin to heal those unresolved emotions; then space opens up for you to see that you were once connected to God. Now is the time to reconnect. It is time to remember who you really are as a spiritual being in a human form having experiencing to help your soul evolve.

Angels Are With You:
You are not alone on your journey. You have many angels, archangels, and spirit guides that are guiding and supporting you along your journey. You just need to ask for their help. God gave us free will. Therefore, the angels cannot do anything to help you until you ask. They will keep nudging you in the right direction, but it is up to you to take the first step and then do the work. There are several ways people are often tempted to block out angelic power. First, people ignore their nudges by over eating to block the gut feelings. Second people ignore their nudges by having such a busy schedule that they do not notice the nudges. Third, people can indulge in alcohol or drugs to quiet their angelic nudges. It is time to start listening to your inner guidance.

There are so many books and stories about angels these days. You may not be able to see your angels at this particular moment, but you might feel or just know that they are around you.

Twenty years ago I started meditating with the intention of seeing and hearing my angels and spirit guides. Every night at the same time for twenty minutes I would sit crossed-legged on the floor staring into the flame of a candle. I focused on my breathing. I would say and do this out loud: *"Breathe in through my nose two, three, four. Hold my breath two, three, four. Exhale out the mouth two, three, four."*

I did this out loud for twenty minutes every night. Every time a thought entered my mind, I would let it go and go back to breathing and counting. It took me twenty-eight days before my spirit guide appeared before my eyes. His name is Juan and he sat crosslegged on the floor in front of me on the other side of the candle. I could see him clearly with my third eye vision.

Then, one by one I could see my guardian angels, Mary and Phillip. I remembered knowing them from earlier in my childhood. It was so great to be able to re-connect with them. I had always felt them around me, but this was better, I could see them and talk to them. We had so much catching up to do. I was so excited.

Over the years, as I have continued mediating daily, my abilities to connect to the spirit realm have grown expeditiously. I am able to see angels, archangels, deceased loved ones, deceased animals, animal totems, and many aspects of other spirit realms.

Connecting with your angels is important because then you can specifically ask for the guidance you need in your every day life. Your angels want so much to help and assist you along your journey.

Starting the Journey:
The questions to ask yourself are: Is my life happy and joyful? Do I create exactly what it is that I want in my life? Am I in the flow of life? Do the doors of the universe just open for me? Do I attract only positive experiences into my life? If you can answer yes to

these questions, then you probably have learned the secrets you need for your life's journey. If you had to answer no to one or more of these questions, than don't you think it is time to start healing so that you can regain your power and recreate what you want in life?

It may seem hard at first, but it does get easier, I promise. When life gets really tough, just ask for more angels to assist you. If it still seems difficult, release your resistance to healing and growing. Then release the resistance that your family may have about your growing. Sometimes your family wants you to stay the way you are because if you change then they may have to look at their own life patterns as well. Many people don't want to change, but would rather live in their dysfunctional patterns.

Technique for Releasing Negative Emotions:

Where in your body do you feel the resistance? This is resistance to change and growth. Where in your body do you store the feelings of fear that stem from your family seeing you grow? What other resistance or fear have you stored in your body? Tune into your body and notice the particular places where you have stored these emotions.

Next, take your hand and pull that blocked or stuck energy out of your body. Use your other hand and pretend the first two fingers are a laser beam and visualize going inside your body and burning off the negative energy. What other negative energy or emotions are stored in your body? Pull them all out and burn off the energy.

Make sure you burn the energy off inside your body. Think of it like this: when you stick a piece of chewing gum to a piece of paper and later try to pull the gum off of the paper part of the gum will remain stuck to the paper. Your negative energy works the same. As you pull the energy out of your body some of it will remain inside your body. Therefore, if you use a laser beam you can go inside your body and burn the remaining energy off so all the negative energy comes out.

Be sure to keep pulling and pulling until you can feel or know that you have gotten all the negative energy out of your body. Next, visualize a gold colored tornado coming down inside the top of your head. Whirling the tornado energy in a clockwise motion, move all the remaining negative energy out of your body. Now make the tornado bigger and push the negative energy out of your auric field (which is the energy around your body). Keep spinning the tornado even bigger. Visualize the tornado moving the negative energy out of your house, out of your city, out of your state. Whirl the negative energy all the way out into space where the universe can recharge it with positive energy.

Last, you want to visualize the color gold coming down inside your body filling you up, head to toe. The angels recommend gold because it is a very high vibration. Whenever you pull negative energy out of your body you will want to fill your body back up with positive energy. If you do not fill back up, you will feel empty inside. Also, leaving an empty space could result in you pulling in negative energy.

General Healing:

The technique demonstrated above works for pulling any negative emotion out of your body. Healing is much easier than we try and make it. Here are the steps for initiating your healing modality:

Step 1: Acknowledge or bring into your awareness the negative emotions you may be experiencing.

Step 2: Own the emotions. Many people are so detached from themselves and their feelings that they are not sure what the emotions are that they are sensing. You must be present in your body in order to own the emotions.

Step 3: Release all the negative emotions. The process outlined above will help you release negative emotions. More techniques for healing will be detailed later on in this book. Such techniques include details on how to release people that you carry and out dated beliefs.

To continue healing keep praying and asking for help, guidance, and direction and then be open to receiving the information whether through a gut feeling, a knowingness, visions, or hearing angelic guidance. Next, learn how to act on that guidance. That gut feeling is your guidance or connection to God and the angels and you just need to trust it. Ask for more specifics or clarity about the information the angels are giving you and then follow it.

Many people recognize that they receive guidance on a daily basis. Often, however, people do not follow that guidance. Guidance comes in different forms. Sometimes you just know things, sometimes you have a gut feeling about something, sometimes you hear their messages and sometimes you have glimpses of the answers you are looking for.

For example, have you ever misplaced your car keys and then suddenly you had a feeling as to where they might be? Have you ever thought about a person and then you hear from them? What about that gut feeling when you just feel something is not quite right? This is all inner guidance from God.

Your angels are here to help you. No job is too small or too big for your angels. I can recall a time that may seem silly to call upon help from the angels, but it was what I needed at the time.

I had taken my sister, Diane out to dinner and a movie for her birthday. When I dropped her off at her house I needed to go to the bathroom but decided I could wait until I got home. It was cold outside and the wind was blowing. I really was just too lazy to get out of the car. I can wait twenty minutes to use the restroom, I convinced myself.

When I got to my gated apartment complex, I pulled out the

cardboard type key card and swiped it in front of the keypad. This was the first time I had ever used my key card. The gates stayed open until 11:00 p.m. every night and re-opened at 6:00 a.m. every morning. I had only lived in this complex a couple of months and had never used my key card before.

To my astonishment, the gate did not open. I flipped the key card over and tried it again. The gate still did not open. Now, I really needed to use the bathroom. I began frantically trying the key card everyway I could think of. It still did not open the gate.

I had been watching for someone else to approach, but no one was in site. I called upon the angels to come and open the gate for me. "Angels, please help me. I need the gate open. I really need to go potty and I am starting to get scared out here in the dark all by myself. Please help me."

Out of nowhere a truck was next to my car. This truck did not drive up, it just appeared. The man in the truck motioned for me to roll my window down. I complied. He told me to turn the key card over. I did and the gate opened. I turned back to thank him, but he was gone. The truck never drove off, it just disappeared.

I quickly drove into my garage and ran into my apartment to use the bathroom. Then I sat down on the couch and realized the full extent of what had just transpired. I gave lots of thanks to the angels. I fully believe that an angel had assumed a human form to give me the information I had asked for and then disappeared.

Angels are definitely with us.

My Connection With God:

Through prayer and meditation I rekindled my connection with God. One day during my meditation, I realized that my cord connecting me to God had three gashes in it. When I asked Archangel Michael what the gashes were about, he explained to me that those were the times when I had given up on God. Those were the times when I was in the dark of the night. I immediately asked Archangel Michael to assist me in repairing those gashes.

Through visualization I was able to see the cord to God fully repaired and connected.

When you meditate you will be able to recognize the importance of mediation or prayer. Meditate on a daily basis. The practice of meditation allows you to stop the resistance and quiet your thoughts. The constant chatter in your head can often consist of negative self-talk. Negative self-talk is a form of resistance to your God-self. The chatter in your head is like a ticker tape that never stops. How would you be able to identify guidance from angels with all that constant chatter? By slowing down your thoughts, you can then pick out the guided information that you are receiving.

It is also very important to observe your thoughts. Are they directed towards what you don't want or are they directed toward what you do want? Most people tend to focus on what they don't want. Then what they don't want shows up in their life. What you focus on is what you get. Start practicing right now focusing on what you want. What are your thoughts? Make it one of your goals to begin to pay attention to your thoughts. Keep them focused on what you want.

You will gain insight and inspiration through your meditation. You can ask for angels, Archangels, Spirit Guides, and Spirit Animals, just to name a few, to assist you. When you learn how to slow your thoughts down, you will be able to access the important information that is given to you by Divine Beings of Light.

Another reason to meditate is to connect to your breathing. According to Dannion Brinkley, the author of *Saved by the Light*, [3] the breath is the means by which we receive guidance and instructions from the spirit world. If you were to watch a baby breathe, you would notice that he/she breathes from a deep place in the belly. Many of us tend to breathe from the upper part of our lungs. This creates a very shallow breath. Instead, when we focus on deep belly breathing, we are connecting into that part of us that is linked to God. Chapter 7 explores another breathing technique and demonstrates additional skills used for meditating.

Why Follow Guidance?:
Being able to following your own inner guidance will help guide you along your soul's journey. Following your inner guidance will make your journey easier. Your inner guidance intuitively knows the road map laid out for this incarnation. Your road map is set for you to grow and learn the lessons you chose to learn this lifetime. When you stray from your map, you exacerbate life's lessons. It is time now to listen to that inner voice of God, is it not? Make the decision to begin now. Listen to your inner wisdom. The more you listen, the more information you will receive. Remember to ask for guidance as well.

Now that you understand the importance of following your inner guidance, you will want to begin your healing journey so that you can receive as much guidance as possible. The more you heal from the old emotional wounds drawn from your past, the easier it will be to gain greater spiritual guidance.

Next, it is time to determine what is holding you back from being all that you can be.

Chapter 6

Discover and Utilize Your Intuition

*"Intuition can be developed by keeping the body, the mind, the soul,
in attunement with the spheres of celestial forces rather than
earthly forces."*

Edgar Cayce

Everyone is born with intuition. Some people do not recognize
that the knowingness that they possess or that the gut feelings
they are experiencing is their intuition. That knowingness inside
of you is your inner connection to Source energy. Source energy
is the same as God or Universal energy.

Intuition is frequently called a hunch or a gut feeling. Some
have even called it a bout of good luck or a burst of genius. It
actually is a function of the right hemisphere of the brain that
involves the extra-sensory perception (ESP). ESP or intuition is
much more because it functions on the physical, emotional,
mental, and spiritual planes of awareness.

Everyone experiences intuition differently. Some people even
experience physical sensations such as tingling of the skin.
Everyone possesses intuition. In our Western culture, however,
women have been conditioned to use it more than men. Your
intuition can be increased once you recognize it and strive to
strengthen, improve, and develop it.

When you take time to be still and quiet your mind, you stop
the resistance from your intellect. This type of resistance
separates you from Source. Therefore, when you are separated
from Source energy, you are not utilizing your intuition which is
yours by birth right.

My Discovery:
When I was twenty-six, my sister took me to see a psychic. Back then, I didn't even know what a psychic was. The woman I went to knew things about me that no one else could possibly know. How did she know what she knew? She used a deck of Tarot cards. When the session was over, I immediately drove to a metaphysical store and bought my first deck of Tarot cards. If she can read Tarot, I thought, so can I.

As I began studying the Tarot, I began developing my intuition more. I had a knowingness of what was happening in someone's life that was deeper than the meaning of the cards I laid out.

As I began looking deeply into my past, I discovered that I had been intuitive all my life. I remember telling my mom things there were going to happen. Mom would tell me that I couldn't say those things. I can even remember being two years old and standing with my hands on my hips says, "You know mom, I am having three kids and no husband."

Mom calmly replied, "No you're not. You have to have a husband first."

I retorted with, "You wait and see, I will have three kids and no husband."

Interestingly, I married, had three kids and then divorced raising all three kids alone. I pointed out to my mother how I was right at age two. I did have kids and no husband.

Mom still did not approve of my knowingness. As I aged, I noticed that by the time I was five years old, I had shut down most of my intuition.

Intuition:
Through your intention, you can learn to expand your awareness and learn to trust the depth of your intuition. You can learn to develop the ability to see, hear, know and feel on intuitive levels. That means that you can learn to discern angels, deceased loved

one, spirit guides, and animal spirits. Sometimes you might possess a knowingness about something. Subsequently, you can learn to recognize that your higher guidance is connecting you to the information that you need to access.

Dr. Doreen Virtue discusses the four clairs of guidance in her book *Divine Guidance.* [1] Doreen states that every person has four methods for receiving Divine guidance:

1. Clairvoyance or clear seeing. This guidance is still pictures or a miniature movie in your mind's eye either inside or outside of your head.
2. Clairaudience which means 'clear hearing,' meaning you hear guidance coming from the outside or from inside your mind.
3. Clairsentience, which is an emotion or a physical sensation.
4. Claircognizance, which is when you just know something. You don't know how you know, but you just know.

Your intuition sends you clear messages in different forms throughout the day. Sometimes your intuition is that gut feeling, when you just feel a gut level awareness. What you sense may include a feeling that you should do something, avoid something, or even follow up on something else.

Because I am primarily an auditory (hearing) person, it has been easy for me to hear the angels that exist in the spirit world.

For example, in 1995 my friend told me there was a good psychic in Estes Park and said I should check her out. I asked Troy, my oldest son, to come with me. We headed down the highway towards Estes Park.

Troy: "Mom, where is this psychic in Estes Park?"

Me: "I don't know specifically only that she is in Estes Park. But don't worry, I will ask Mary, my guardian angel, to direct us when we get to the city."

Troy: "Ok,"

As we drove into the city, Troy said, "Well let me know where to go."

Mary (my guardian angel): "Turn left here."

So we did. Troy began heading up a street.

All of a sudden I heard Mary say: "Slow down, you went too far. Troy drives much too fast."

Troy does drive fast and since neither one of us had ever been to Estes Park, slowing down was an excellent idea.

Mary: "You passed it, turn around."

Mary: "Now turn right here and then right into the parking lot and find a place to park." We did as she said.

Mary: "Now, go inside and ask the first person you see where the psychic is located. She is somewhere in this building."

I walked up to a man I saw and asked him if he knew of a psychic located in this building. He said, "Yes, she is down the hall on the left."

Trusting the information you obtain allows you to access even more information. Everyone is intuitive. Some people may be more intuitive than others, but that is because they ask for information and then recognize when they get the answer. When you use your intuition on a daily basis it gets stronger. Raising your vibration through cleaning up your past issues helps you to receive the guidance from the angels more clearly on a daily basis.

Clearing the Past:

People often possess beliefs that keep them from trusting their inherent intuition. Sometimes you have a fear of what others might say if they knew you believed in psychic abilities. It is time to discover what beliefs and patterns are keeping you from completely opening to your full potential. Begin making a list of all the beliefs that you have that are keeping you for trusting your intuition.

Inner Knowingness:

Your intuition can come to you in many different forms such as: seeing, hearing, feeling, and knowing. Therefore, you want to begin by understanding how you already receive your guidance. Pay attention to your inner knowingness and determine if you feel things, sense things, or just know things. Those are the ways in which most people receive various degrees of inner guidance.

I rarely run across someone that has hearing like I have. I think I over developed my hearing in my childhood as a means of protection because of the abuse I received from my father. At the same time, I shut down my gut feelings. I didn't like feeling the abuse or other negative emotions. I tuned into my knowingness and hearing for survival.

When I started enhancing my psychic abilities, I had to spent time practicing feeling and sensing things. I started by sitting in a room and tuning into the energy of the room. I also practiced feeling and sensing the energy around crystals. Today, I still have to work at feeling. It is so much easier for me to just know something or to hear the voices of the spirit world than to tune into the sensations received by my body and gut awareness.

Examples of Knowingness:

Think of a time when you were driving and you just had a feeling that you needed to slow down because a policeman was waiting up ahead. Sure enough, a block or so later, you spot the policeman running radar.

What about the times when you just have this knowingness that it would be faster to take a certain route home from work? Later you hear there had been an accident on the road you usually take.

Remember the times your phone has rang and you just knew who was on the other end of the line before you even picked the phone up. Those are examples of your intuition.

Telepathy:

Telepathy is also a form of intuition. My granddaughter calls it "mind talk." Notice how often you think of someone and then they call. I have some great examples of telepathy. I raised my three kids to practice and use telepathy. It was not uncommon for me to get messages from them on a regular basis.

When my daughter, Sonia, was in high school, she and I would go to a Mexican restaurant that we had grown to love. My boys had already graduated and moved out. One day I was driving home from work and I knew in my mind that Sonia wanted to have dinner at our favorite Mexican restaurant. She was sending me telepathy messages. I sent back a message to her that I had clients and would not have time. Sonia sent back to me the message that we did have enough time. I sent back to her the message that I didn't think there was enough time. She sent back to me the message that she would be waiting in the garage for me and we were definitely going.

Sure enough, I pulled into the garage and she was standing there with a big grin on her face. Her first words were: "Mom, we have plenty of time, they have such fast service, and we will be fine."

Sherry's Control Telepathy:

My best friend, Sherry, wanted to learn telepathy many years ago. Sherry wanted to know how to do telepathy because she saw how my kids and I used it all the time. I explained to her how to do it. You just picture the person in your mind and then tell them what you want them to know. This is an easy exercise to perform.

Sherry knew a guy at work, Will, which she wanted to practice telepathy on. One night she spent two hours visualizing Will. Sherry wanted to see if she could telepathy to him and if he would get it. So, she decided that she would visualize Will in a blue shirt to see if Will would wear a blue shirt to work the next day. However, while she was visualizing this, Sherry realized that he looked really good in red as well and then could not make up her mind on what color of shirt she wanted him to wear. She spent two hours visualizing Will in red and then blue, then red and then blue.

Can you guess what color of shirt he wore to work the next day? Blue. But, it doesn't stop there. The next day he wore red and then blue and then red and then blue. This went on for two weeks. It was so funny. She tired of the red and blue shirts and started visualizing him in a different color every night. The next morning she would call me to tell me that he wore the color she had visualized.

There have been numerous times when I wanted to get a hold of one of my kids and I would send them a telepathy message to call me. Within a few minutes they would call.

Can you see now how you have used telepathy in your life? If you haven't used telepathy in the past, begin practicing. Now, you do not need to go to the extremes that my friend Sherry did. Just start by picturing a family member in your mind. Tell that person that you want to talk to them. Avoid doing it from control, as that will come back to haunt you.

Sherry's story with Will ended up badly because she became controlling. She got bored with the shirt colors and started willing him to ask her out. Every night she spent an hour or so visualizing and telling him to ask her out. After a week, he went from flirting and talking to her to totally ignoring her. Sherry was trying to control this man. He picked up on her control issues and exercised his free will to walk away. We all have free will.

Intuitive Guidance:
Expect intuitive or psychic guidance. Your intention sets the

pace, "I am open to my intuition." When you say those words, do you feel open to receiving guidance? Do you have any fears about receiving such guidance? Some of my clients have mentioned that they were afraid they would get information that they couldn't handle. If this is your thought, then you are blocking some aspect of your intuitive guidance.

Begin clearing out any out dated or old beliefs that are preventing you from tuning into your higher guidance. Many children see angels and spirits. Because they do not know what or who they are, these spirits often scare them. Children often shut down their psychic abilities due to their fears. Are you one of those children?

I read an interesting article that goes like this:

"Marine Corps Lieutenant General Paul Van Riper believed the best way to make decisions was to frame a problem, collect data, formulate alternatives, and then evaluate the options. Almost every organization that trains decision-makers has followed the same approach. But General Van Riper learned that these methods don't work in actual combat.

Inspired by cognitive psychologist Gary Klein's work with firefighters, who have to make life and death decisions quickly, General Van Riper brought his Marines to the New York Mercantile Exchange in 1995, because the jostling, confusing pits reminded him of war rooms during combat. To no one's surprise, the Marines did not fare as well as the traders. But when the General brought the traders to the Marine's base to play war games, he and many others were amazed when the traders trounced the Marines at war! When the Marines analyzed the humbling results, they concluded that the traders were better 'gut thinkers.' Thoroughly practiced at quickly evaluating risks, they were far more willing to act decisively on the kind of imperfect and contradictory information that is all you get in war.

Today the Corp's official doctrine reads, 'The intuitive approach is more appropriate for the vast majority of ... decisions made in the fluid, rapidly changing conditions of war when time and uncertainty are critical factors, and creativity is a desirable trait.'"[2] This article shows how important gut feelings or intuition are. Some of our military leaders are now recognizing the important of higher guidance.

According to Edgar Cayce's readings, "intuitive influences come more from the soul than merely from the mental activities of an entity." He says that "intuition can be developed by keeping the body, the mind, the soul, in attunement with the spheres of celestial forces rather than earthly forces." A "closer communion with the spirituality of things, peoples, conditions, and circumstances will gradually make for the development of intuitive influences."[3]

Cayce discusses how one just needs to practice and tune into the inner knowingness that is inside you. Cayce also mentions that one must "know thyself," stay close to Source, and trust what comes from within.

Intuition Environment:
William Kautz, Director of the Center for Applied Intuition of San Francisco, California states that the intuition stems from the superconscious mind. In order to reach the conscious mind, it must travel through the subconscious where it may be distorted by fears, memories, and impressions stored there.

Research gathered from Center for Applied Intuition of San Francisco has indicated that physical environment can enhance or inhibit intuition. "An ideal intuition enhancing room is painted light green, aqua, or chartreuse; lit with natural sunlight that keeps the temperature between 70 and 73 degrees Fahrenheit with the humidity between 60 and 70 percent. Also, music stimulates intuition by putting an individual in a relaxed state to produce pleasant memories, which cause the right and left hemispheres of the brain to work in greater unity. The presence of plants cleanses the air of pollutants." [4]

Jung's Perception:

Within the realm of psychology, intuition has drawn much attention. Psychiatrist Carl G. Jung described intuition as "a perception of realities which are not known to the conscious, and which goes via the unconscious." [5] Jung continued to state his belief that the intuition is not merely a perception, but a creative process with the capacity to inspire.

Moreover, Jung depicts humans as being oriented to the world by four functions: sensation, feeling, thinking, and intuition. The latter gives information concerning both future possibilities and the atmosphere surrounding all experiences: archetypes are inborn forms of intuition. (This coincides with Jung's theory of the collective conscious.) Jung employed four types that classify particular psychological types. Basically, they include the extroverted and the introverted. Those that are extroverted are mostly materialistic; living their lives with little respect for law or custom or feelings of others. They squander their energies while living in the world of reality. On the other hand, the introverted tend to be artists, mystics, seers, and prophets and are tuned into the tenets of the collective unconscious. They frequently appear strange to others.[6]

Intuition is an important aspect of mysticism. It is thought to be vital in the perception of direct and immediate truths pertaining to the most intimate secrets of life. Through deep mediation, mystics experience intuitive flashes in which they perceive the ineffable nature of the cosmos, the Divine Force, the soul, and the unity of all.

Throughout history cultures have had intuitive leaders. For example, Native Americans relied on the insights of the Shamans. Aztec cultures relied on High Priestess and Shamans. Further historical studies reflect how people have relied on intuitive guidance through the course of their lives. Biblical scriptures, including the Dead Sea Scrolls, are riddled with talks of intuitive guidance. Most cultures have relied on this necessary form of spiritual insight to guide them on life's journey.

Chapter 7

How Other People's Energy Affects You

'Energy cannot be created or destroyed, it just changes form.'
Albert Einstein

Once you begin to trust in your own intuition, you must also be competent enough to discern the difference between your feelings and energy that you are drawing from other people.

Most people realize that they are able to read body language or the language encoded within a room. You may not think about doing it or that you can, but it is a normal occurrence to read others. Body language comprises up to about 50 percent or more of what we express or communicate to others.

While reading other people's body language many people are also decoding basic feelings, thoughts, and observations. You can do that through watching their body language, or decoding and interpreting verbal speech patterns. Thus, intuition has an important role to play.

Michael's Energy:
I have discovered how empathic I really am. I did not realize until about four years ago the degree to which I absorb other people's thoughts, feelings, and ideas. I divorced Michael four years ago. We remained friends. One day my garbage disposal broke and he offered to come over to replace it for me. Michael had been in the house twenty minutes when I started having thoughts like: "I still love you. We can work things out. We need to be together."

I realized my thoughts and wondered why I was thinking

these words. I excused myself and went upstairs to the bathroom. I cleaned off my energy, re-grounded, cleaned out my head. I checked inside my heart and knew that I could not want to be with Michael. With my energy cleared and balanced, I went back downstairs.

Under the sink, Michael was pulling out the old garbage disposal so we could go to Home Depot and get a new one. I sat on the floor next to him to give him tools. Within a few minutes, I started feeling the exact same feelings and thoughts. My head started telling me that I loved him and wanted to work things out.

I found this to be a very strange occurrence. I left the kitchen again and went back upstairs. I re-cleared my energy, my head, and my heart. Did I really love him and want to work things out? No. So, what was going on?

With unwanted energy once again reprogrammed, I returned to the task downstairs. The disposal was out and we were ready to go to Home Depot. I started feeling those feelings and thoughts come crashing down after we had been in the truck only a few minutes. They emotions were so strong that tears came to my eyes.

Once inside the store, I walked behind Michael a few feet so that I could re-ground and clear my energy. We found the disposals. I started having feelings of wanting to hug Michael. Instead of hugging him, I told him I would be right back that there was something else in the store that I wanted to look at.

By now, I was really getting really disturbed with myself. How could this keep occurring? We went home and he stayed with me for four more hours. I had to leave the room every 20-30 minutes to clear my energy. On a couple of occasions the emotions were so strong I just started crying. He didn't know what was wrong and neither did I, at least not at first.

Finally, I figured everything out. I was reading all of Michael's thoughts and feelings. When I was away from him, it was very clear to me that I did not want to get back together. I was clear that I was not in love with him.

This was a huge lesson for me. I realized for the first time just how empathic I was. I picked up all of Michael's thoughts and feelings. Many times people begin to feel different emotions that they assume is a part of their agenda. But in reality, those feelings may very well originate from others.

Assuming Allie's Energy:

Since I discovered how empathic I was, I began really paying attention to my intuition. When Allie, my granddaughter, was born I kept her during the day while her parents worked. I could do readings and care for her at the same time. When she was about nine months old, she caught an upper respiratory infection.

I was holding Allie and within minutes I started experiencing a tightness in my chest and congestion. I simply didn't feel good. I immediately realized that this range of symptoms were all a part of Allie's symptoms. I pulled her energy out of my body and pictured a titanium wall between us so that I would not absorb her illness. Since that time, I have learned how easily I pick up other people's energies.

Clearing Out Other's Energy:

Have you ever been to a mall and within a short period of time you were exhausted? What has happened here is that you began absorbing the energy of the mall and all the people in it. Everyone absorbs energy whether you realize it or not. Start noticing how you get more tired in crowds than you do when in the privacy of your own home.

Next time you go to work begin to observe how you absorb the energy of the people around you in the work place. Notice how you can feel what they are experiencing. The only way to begin to manage your energy is to start with noticing the difference between your energy and other people's energy.

Start with cleaning your energy out. There are several energy clearing methods to use. One method is as follows:

Take your hand with your palm facing your body. Bend your fingers like you are going to scratch yourself. Now scrape your energy starting at your head and moving down to your toes. You do not touch your body. Keep your fingers about a half inch away from your body. Do your whole body. Notice how you can feel the difference? You can feel the yucky energy coming off your body.

Next, pretend that a gold tornado or whirlwind is coming down inside your body and pushing all the negative energy out of your body. Make the tornado bigger and bigger. Push the negative energy out of your body, out of your auric field, out of your house, out of your city, out of your state, and all the way out into the universe. The universe takes this negative energy and recharges it into positive energy.

Finally, you want to clear out your head. Go inside your head and tell everyone in there that they must leave. No one should be in your head but you. Demand everyone to leave your head. Get all the people out. Get all the negative thoughts out. It does not mean that you do not love your mom or your spouse; it just means that no one should be in your head but you.

After you have everyone out of your head, then you can put a chair in the middle of your head and you can sit in the chair looking out your own eyes. You can even decorate your head with colors like blue, green, teal, etc.

Now you want to put a protective bubble around you. Make sure you clean your energy field first, so as not to trap negative energy into your field. Using the tornado step mentioned above will clean out your energy field. I use the color gold (I will explain why in a minute). Picture the gold bubble around you in a circle about three to four feet in diameter. Then on the outside of the gold bubble, I put a 2 inch layer of titanium. This titanium really keeps other people's energy out of your space.

Now that your energy has been cleared, go out to a store or mall. Pay close attention to everything that you begin to feel, see, know, and sense. What vibrations are you picking up? Notice how you are beginning to feel differently than when you first walked into the store. Are you starting to get heavy or tired? What emotions are beginning to impact your psyche?

You will have to repeat this exercise throughout the day. It only takes a minute. You will want to put the same protective bubble around your house and your car. Notice how you can even pick up other people's energy while you are driving. Really sensitive people can feel the energy that has been on the road long before you began driving that path. Negative energy stays in the energy field for a very long time.

The first time I drove from Denver to Canada, I remember having a hard time with some of the energy that I encountered. I was with a friend, Rosemary, and we were going to Canada to participate in a Metaphysical Fair. Driving through Wyoming, as we began to approach the northern part of the state, I started feeling really heavy. Then, I started having visions of Indians and white men fighting. I could perceive all the fear and death. I told Rosemary what I was feeling and she explained to me it was because we were near the site of the battle of Custer's Last Stand.

I didn't care for history in school, so I had no knowledge of what had occurred. Once Rosemary explained everything to me it made complete sense. Although the battle took place a long time ago, I still perceive it whenever I drive through Wyoming.

When you can learn to discern what is your energy and what is not, then you can begin to manage your energy better. It is important to be able to understand when you are picking up other people's energy, thoughts, and feelings. Being sensitive to others' vibration can sometimes be exhilarating or inconvenient depending on the circumstances.

Using Gold:
Archangel Michael guided me to use gold as protection instead of white. White attracts dark. I kept attracting entities (deceased people that have not crossed over) to me.

Here is one example of how a white bubble affected me. I was driving from Denver to Crestone, Colorado to do a weekend Metaphysical Fair. As I turned off the highway towards Crestone, I made sure my white bubble was around me.

About ten miles west of Crestone, I started seeing visions of the Indians attacking a wagon train. I could hear the screams of various people being killed. I could feel the hair on the back of my neck stand up.

As I settled into my hotel, I could feel all the negative energy swarming around the room and permeating the hotel. I cleaned my room with a smudge stick. It did not help.

Later, I went to dinner in a restaurant in town. Once again, I started having more visions of Indian and white man's battles all along the mountains that extend all the way to Crestone. While the scenery is incredibly beautiful in Crestone, I was having a hard time enjoying it because of all the deceased people and all their trapped negative energy.

I woke up the next morning hoarse and congested. Later I became ill with an upper respiratory infection. I could hardly wait to leave on Sunday night. When I got home, I called my son, Troy, and had him come over to clean my energy off and remove the two entities that had attached themselves to my body.

The following year I went back to Crestone, but I actually stated in a hotel in Salida and drove the 40-minute drive to Crestone. I did the fair during the day and drove back to Salida at night. I was able to handle the negative energy better that way.

After that event, Archangel Michael explained to me that because I am so sensitive I should use the gold bubble with a two inch titanium layer on the outside of the gold bubble. I have never had any problems with picking up entities since I started using the gold. I am able to manage my energy better and keep other people's negative energy out of my space more efficiently.

Archangel Jewelry:

In December of 2007, the archangels revealed to me that I would be designing jewelry to assist people. The angels woke me during the night and explained to me how to make the jewelry utilizing Swarovski crystals. The angels further explained that they would infuse their sacred energy into each piece of jewelry so that when a person wears a particular piece, he/she can connect to the angelic and ascended master realm. All of the bracelets and necklaces absorb and repel negative energy. In addition, each piece of jewelry has extended specific benefits that are connected to each angel and ascended master.

First, I made a Melchizedek bracelet for me to wear. I do a lot of Metaphysical fairs every year. I always felt so tired by the end of the day because of all of the negative energy I would constantly absorb. The first time I wore my Melchizedek bracelet at a first fair, I was totally shocked. I did not get tired at all. My energy felt vibrant. The beads on my Melchizedek bracelet were almost black. They had started out with pink, yellow, crystal clear, and blue. Due to the unique vibration, my bracelet absorbed all of the negative energy. I personally did not any negative energy. It was wonderful. I wear at least two or three different bracelets every day. I see a big difference in my energy from wearing these archangel and ascended master jewelry as well as utilizing the gold bubble. To view the collection of Archangel and Ascended Master jewelry, visit my website at www.alternativechanges.com.

Balancing:

It is important to clean and balance your energy and chakras on a regular basis. The next chapter gives you step by step instructions on how to accomplish this. You will also discover more techniques on how to block other people's negative energies and details as to how to clean out your own energetic patterns.

Clearing Your House:

Everyone's house picks up negative energy just like you do. When people come to your house, they leave their energy. Should there be any fighting or negative energy between spouses and children, you have negative energy. Your house absorbs energy just like people; therefore, you need to clean your house.

The angels told me many years ago to use yellow curry powder to clean my house. You can buy yellow curry in the spice section of your grocery store. The purpose for using yellow curry is to dissolve the negative energy.

You put 2-3 tablespoons of curry powder in a pan of water. Use a large pot and only fill it up part way. Curry stains whatever it touches, so be careful not to spill it. Once the water starts boiling, you will see the steam. After the curry has boiled a minute or two creating lots of steam, then carefully carry the pan to your first room to clean. Hold the pan on the floor in the corners of the room for thirty seconds or so. Let the steam rise in the corner cleaning out the negative energy. After all four corners are complete, the set the pan in the middle of the room. You will begin to see, sense, feel, or know how the negative energy is being transformed.

Once this room is completely cleaned, put the pan back on the stove. The water needs to boil again in order to get the steam flowing. You can add water as needed. Next, continue with each room in your house. Then you can just leave the pot on the stove letting it boil. This will continue cleaning the main part of your house. Remember to add water and more curry if you feel that all the curry has boiled away.

You will notice how peaceful your house feels. You will want to clean your house as often as it needs. I have lots of people coming and going through my house; therefore, I clean my house every week. If you do not have as much negative energy in your house, you will not need to clean as often.

I live in a two-storey with a basement and clean all three levels. If you house is not as negative, you can just put the pan on the stove and let it boil. You may not need to do each room individually as often if you live alone.

The angels taught me to use yellow curry powder instead of a smudge stick because the curry dissipates the negative energy. If you watch the energy of a smudge stick, the negative energy goes into the corners of a room and then later starts filtering back out into the room. The smudge stick does not dissipate the negative energy. In addition, smudge sticks mess up my sinuses.

Should you use a smudge stick, be sure to open all the windows and doors and move the energy out of the house.

PART III:

Healing Modalities

"Things do not change; we change."
Henry David Thoreau

Chapter 8

Techniques for Making Changes

"Finish each day and be done with it. You have done
what you could."
Ralph Waldo Emerson

This chapter demonstrates additional methods to help you gain control over your own space. In addition, you will discover how to release negative emotions that you have stored in your body. You may want to start the process by writing in a journal every night that will reveal your inner most thoughts. Start noticing the things that are blocking your energy. Go back over your childhood and the emotions that you know you are still holding onto. The journaling is one way to start getting in touch with your inner feelings and ascertain core issues.

Once a month you can burn those pages as a ceremony of letting go. Journaling will reveal a wide variety of emotions that you are now ready to bring into your awareness. Writing down the events helps you to own the emotions. Subsequently, you will want to release the emotions through the different techniques described in the book.

Because everyone is different, you want to find the processes that work best for you. As you work with the various tools, you will discover how powerful they all are. You will also begin to notice how I have activated all these tools so as to open you up to the highest vibrational levels possible.

Now that I have been releasing and healing for many years, I do not always take the time to journal exactly what I am feeling in every instance. Usually, I find that I am instantly aware of what is going on inside of me. I acknowledge my emotions and immediately release them. I do not want to spend time carrying negative emotions in my body and getting bogged down. My energy needs to be clear so that I can help others and do my work.

Also, I want to mention that many people have brought in past life baggage such as vows, curses, hexes, and karma that will need to be cleared. At the same time, you will want to clear any ancestral patterns that are blocking you.

Please recognize that any time you attract someone into your life, you should look at their behaviors and see which ones are being mirrored back to you. The behaviors that you like are mirroring the things you like about yourself. The behaviors you do not admire are also mirrors of your own personality. Search inside to find the negative mirrors.

For example, if you have controlling people in your life, where are you controlling? If you notice that others complain a lot, see if you complain a lot. If you do not complain, then who in your childhood was the complainer? If it was your mom, then her complaining created a specific wound within. You will attract other people that complain giving you the opportunity to forgive your mom for her complaining. Until you heal that wound, you keep attracting it to you.

Before you start your healing process, I should offer a disclaimer here. It takes a lot of energy to suppress the intensity of negative emotions. Therefore, when you begin releasing these pent up emotions it can cause a mild case of diarrhea, headache and other types of exhaustive tiredness. Usually the side effects are short term (24-48 hours). I have discovered that if you take an Epsom salt bath after doing a major clearing, the bath is successful in pulling the toxins out of your body. Thus, the side effects will be minimal, if any.

I typically take an Epsom salts bath weekly to keep the toxins out of my body. Use 1-2 cups of Epsom salts in a warm bath and soak for 20-30 minutes. You can use this time to scan your body for any cords or any other energy blocks that might be keeping you out of balance.

In addition, bruising is a common way for your body to release pent up emotions. As you heal, just notice if you have any unusual marks on your body that seem to creep up out of nowhere. Your body does hold memories of energy patterns. Therefore, the marks can be the result of you releasing such pent up emotions.

One of my clients, Kathy, experienced black and blue marks around her eyes. She also had minor cuts on her wrist and marks on her neck. They appeared at the time we began healing the emotions from her childhood traumas.

What we discovered in her past was sexual and physical abuse. The man that abused her hit her causing black eyes. The abusive man also put Kathy in frequent choke holds creating hand prints and bruises on her neck and throat. The cuts on her wrists were from the times this man took a razor blade to her. Discovering the traumas in Kathy's past that had been suppressed made perfect sense as to why her body was releasing the exact marks as we were healing those events and emotions.

Grounding into Your Body:

The first thing you want to do is to learn to ground into your body. Grounding will help you stay in your body so that you can be present to meet with life's challenges. Many people do not recognize that their spirit is partially out of their body until I point it out to them. What happens is your feet are up around your chest and the rest of you is above your body. You are still attached to your body so it can function, but typically you are not present.

Have you ever felt spacey, zoned out, or day dreamy? Do you ever feel over-whelmed, light-headed, or disconnected? Those are the times that you are not fully grounded into your body. When you are not present and not consciously aware of your body, notice how spacey or light-headed you feel. You will have a tendency to bump into walls and furniture when out of your body. You will forget where you put things. You will not be paying attention when someone is talking to you. Do you recognize any of this behavior? Let's get in your body. You can quickly do so by jumping up and down and feeling yourself move all the way down into your toes. You can use your intention to get back into your body as well.

Everyone leaves their body at night. During the day, however, many of you come and go. Thus, begin to pay attention and see if you are in or out of your body and whether you are fully grounded. As you pay attention to this, you will learn to recognize when you are in or out of your body.

When you are present in your body, you are able to feel your emotions. This will enable you to heal these unresolved emotions that are blocking you from being in a state of peace. Also when you are grounded and have cleared the blockages out of your body, you can create the things you want in your life and actually get them.

One of the reasons you do not enjoy being in your body is because of all the unresolved emotional baggage that feels so heavy. The baggage is blocked energy. That blocked energy can create illness. If your body is ill, you will not enjoy being inside your body. So clearing out the blocked energy will actually enable you to enjoy your body more. Realize that major unresolved emotions stored in your body as a child show up as illness as an adult.

Many of our children spend a lot of time outside of their bodies. The reason for this is because they are not accustomed to having a body since they did not have one before they come to earth. When our kids go to school and become bored, they often leave their body. Leaving their body means they are not present enough to absorb the information being taught to them. These kids end up getting labeled ADD and ADDHD. If you would just clean off their energy and teach them to ground, then they would be more present.

To quickly clean off your child or yourself you simply start at your head and brush your body with your hand. For example, lightly brush or scrape (as discussed earlier) your head, neck, arms, chest, and back while you are saying:

"God, please remove from me all negative energy mentally, physically, emotionally and spiritually. "

After this exercise, notice if you have any cords attached to you. If so, quickly pull the cords. (The instructions on cord pulling are a little farther down in this chapter.) Perform the same process on your children. You will notice an immediate change in their energy and your own.

My two little granddaughters often will leave their bodies. It has become a joke around my house when I tell them to get back into their bodies. My two-year old granddaughter told me just the other day to get back into my body. I was taking her to pre-school and missed the turn because I was out of body and not paying attention. I literally forgot where I was going until she hollered at me. We both laughed.

The girls both fall a lot or bump into things and get hurt. I realize it is because they are not fully in their bodies. I remind them frequently to get all the way down into their toes so that they know where their bodies are so they can relate to the physical world in an appropriate way.

Jumping up and down for a child is a quick and easy way to be able to ground. As an adult, you can firmly stomp your feet and use your intention to get back into your body in a different and more sophisticated way.

You can also use this technique to ground every morning so that you can get back into your body and set the energy for the entire day. Then throughout the day you can use either technique. Sit down in a comfortable chair. Take a couple of deep breaths. Breathe in through the nose and out through the mouth.

As you breathe in through your nose, count one, two, three, four. Hold your breath for a count of one, two, three, four.

Then, exhale out your mouth to a count of one, two, three, four, five, six, seven and eight. You always exhale more than you inhale as this gets all the excess air out of your lungs. Breathe into the belly. Do this a couple of times in order to help you relax.

Now, picture an old oak tree trunk going from your tailbone all the way down into the earth. Keep going all the way down to the center of the earth. Your tailbone area is your root chakra. Push this tree trunk through all the layers of the earth all the way down to the center of the earth. Now visualize the big old rock at the center of the earth. Spread the roots of your old oak tree out and either bury the roots, velcro the roots down, glue them, or whatever works for you.

Notice as you ground the roots that you can feel a tug that draws you downward into your body. You should now be looking out through your eyes. Make the tree trunk as wide as your hips. Your tree trunk is called your grounding cord. Next, put today's date on the tree trunk so that you are grounded in present time.

Now, place an imaginary release button on the grounding cord. Turn it towards the 'on' position. You do all of this using your mind's eye. The purpose of the release button is to find a way of releasing all the nervous energy from your body down through the grounding cord into mother earth. Mother earth loves this used energy. Mother earth recycles the energy and sends it back up re-charged to be used again.

After you have a complete understanding of the use of the grounding cord, then you can play with it. You can make your grounding cord out of anything you want. It can be a beam of light, a slide, or whatever your imagination can come up with. As long as you connect it down into the big rock in the center of the earth and feel the tug pulling you back inside your body, you can use whatever grounding cord works for you.

You will want to be aware of when you are out of your body (ungrounded) so that you can re-ground (be present) throughout the day. You do not need to sit down to ground. You can visualize a grounding cord in your minds' eye in less than two seconds no matter where you are. Or, if you are in a place that you can stamp your feet to get back into your body, this works really well. This does take practice.

In my daily morning meditation, I perform this entire process of grounding, putting a date on my cord, and then a release button. Then, throughout the day, I pay attention as to whether or not I am in my body.

Another technique is to put one hand on your heart chakra and the other hand on your belly (solar plexus chakra). Feel the heat and energy stemming from these two chakras. This practice will place you in your body, but you need to assure that you are in your toes. You will want to really feel your body to be sure that you are all the way inside it.

Other people's energy and different environments will throw you out of your body. Being aware of whether you are grounded (being in your body) or not is the first step to self-awareness. Once you have grounded a couple of times you can do this anywhere in a few valuable seconds. This means you will be more present to yourself and others. What a difference grounding can make to your self-realization and balance.

When your spirit is out of your body, the body does not receive energy. Hence you may feel tired. I had a client that I noticed was partially out of body. It appeared her feet were up around her chest. I knew she had not fully been in her body for at least twenty years. When I taught her how to ground, she said, "I finally understand why my feet and legs have been numb for all these years." Because she did not ground, she had no energy, therefore, no feelings.

Ground Others:

Every day during my morning meditation I ground my house and yard. I ground my two kittens as well. They are two years old and a little rowdy, running through the house, knocking things over. So, I picture a grounding cord about a foot below their tails and watch them latch onto it. They instantly change their behavior and slow way down. They will still play and wrestle with each other, but they do it on the floor instead of leaping off of tables and furniture.

I took care of my youngest granddaughter during the first year of her life. When she would get upset and cry, I would simply picture a grounding cord a foot below her tailbone and she would latch onto it and immediately calm down.

You can even use this technique during staff meetings. You can ground the room and then your co-workers so that meetings are more productive. To ground your co-workers, you want to picture a grounding cord a foot below your co-workers' tailbones. Make the cord as wide as their hips and watch the energy shift immediately. Most of the people will automatically attach to the grounding cord. Subsequently, ground the room by picturing a large tree trunk as big as the room and ground it all the way down into the center of the earth.

I fly a lot and always ground the airplane so that it is safe especially during storms and turbulence. Play with this and see how it can work for you.

Understanding Your Energy:

Next, you may want to learn how to place boundaries around your energy field (aura) so that you do not continue picking up other people's energy field. How many times have you gone somewhere and felt totally drained after just a few minutes? I used to have a hard time going into a shopping mall because I would be drained after a few minutes. I am very empathic and tend to pick up other people's energy. This was a problem for me because my daughter loves to shop. After five minutes, I would feel exhausted and I would need to leave the mall.

I am a high-energy person and for a long time could never figure out why shopping exhausted me so quickly. What I learned was that malls create a lot of noise and distractions to un-ground you so that you spend more money. I would get in a mall and be so un-grounded and start feeling all these strange emotions that I would buy things that I did not originally go to the mall for. While this is an excellent ploy for the stores, it was not good for my budget and my spiritual developement.

Now that I have learned to ground and set my boundaries, I can shop for several hours if I want to. I do have to keep grounding and setting my boundaries throughout the day, but I do it in my mind's eye in just a matter of seconds so it does not interfere with my activities.

How are you at family gatherings? Do you leave feeling totally drained? Perhaps you feel angry or depressed. Perhaps any number of additional emotions may have been picked up from your family. Were you initially feeling fine before you went to meet your family? Later, after just a short period of time did you feel somewhat drained? It is because you picked up their energy and took it on as if it were your own.

Has your spouse ever come home in a bad mood and within a few minutes you are also in a bad mood, when prior to that, you were perfectly happy? Can you differentiate between your energy, thoughts and feelings and those of your spouse or family? I am naturally a very happy person. After talking to my sister for a few minutes I used to find myself down in the dumps. I did not understand or recognize what the cause or solution was for many years.

Currently, though, I have learned how to clear out other people's energy and in order to keep my own space clean. It is very important to learn to do this so that you are not thrown off balance so easily by other people's energy. Setting your grounding cord is the first step to remedy the situation. Follow the rest of the steps to set boundaries and clear your energy so that you can remain a vibrant, healthy, and joyful individual.

Setting Your Boundaries:
Picture a rose four-foot tall out in front of you. Place it out about three-feet away from you. The rose can be any color you want. The flower should be open and you can have a couple of smaller roses on the same stem if it feels like you need them. With your intention, you would need to call your energy back towards the three-foot rose in front of you.

Some people's energy is all the way across the room, while others have their energy just a couple of feet out in front of them. I have even seen some people that have their energy all the way around the globe. Just notice where your energy is. Now, with your intention, bring your energy, which is your aura, back to the rose out in front of you.

If your energy is closer than three-feet, push it out to three-feet. You pick up everything that is in your energy field. Therefore, if your energy goes around the globe, you are taking on and owning all the surrounding negative emotions from other people. In that respect, you may become too drained physically and emotionally. By bringing your energy within the three-foot boundary, your energy is much more manageable.

If your energy is right up next to your body, it is too stifling and closed in. It does not allow you to breathe and grow. You can handle the energy of a three-foot circle without feeling so overwhelmed.

Next, you are going to put another rose directly behind your body out three-feet. Now, put one on your left side and one on your right side all three-feet out. These roses can all be the same color or different colors, that part is irrelevant. Next, put a rose above your head and then place one below your feet as well.

Now, you have six roses around you. If for some reason a rose does not seem to work for you, then pick a flower that does. I use roses because they have some sacredness Biblical aspects to them. Also, the rose can hold and collect a lot of negative energy.

Next, I want you to ground all six roses all the way down into Mother Earth. Ground them all the way down to the center of the earth going through all the layers of the earth to get there. Root them well and be sure they are securely grounded just like you did with your grounding cord.

Throughout the day, if you are picking up a lot of negative energy, you will notice that your roses will wilt. Just send them down into the earth and create new roses.

The next step is to picture a big golden sun above your head with a magnet in the center of it. This magnet brings all your scattered energy back to you. People leave energy at work, in the car, at the store, at your parent's house, just to name a few places.

Picture this big golden sun above your head and put a magnet in the center. Then visualize your energy coming back to you filling up the sun and making it even bigger. When your sun is nice and full, mentally bring it down and fill up your body head to toe. Then spread the gold energy out to the roses filling up the three-foot circle with gold energy. Bring the golden energy all the way down to the ground and below the earth a foot tucking it into your grounding cord.

You are now sitting inside a gold bubble that is three-feet in diameter. What happens is when someone's negative energy starts coming towards you, it hits the roses or the gold bubble and the gold acts like a deflector sending their negative energy down into mother earth to be re-cycled and brought back up as positive energy. The roses act as a boundary.

I add a two-inch thick layer of titanium over my gold bubble as added protection. I am very empathic and this helps me to not pick up other people's energy so quickly. If you feel the gold bubble is enough that is perfect.

This will not block all negative energy; however, it will

certainly get most of it and the next steps will clear the rest. Also, now you only have a three-foot circle to keep clean and be responsible for instead of a whole neighborhood or more.

This process helps you learn to set boundaries with your own energy and makes it more manageable to keep clean. If you are picking up other people's energy, you are probably inside their space or allowing them in your space. It is important to learn that you are only responsible for your space.

You can visualize your children inside a gold bubble, if they are too young to do this process themselves. Many times at the fairs I work, parents come with their little ones. The kids get overwhelmed with all the different energy in these crowds and they start crying. If you just take a few minutes before going into a crowded place and ground them, put roses around them, and then add the golden sun, you will be surprised at how much better they behave when they are not being bombarded by energy. Remember, if all that energy is hard on you, your children are usually a lot more sensitive than you are and experience even more acutely what you yourself are experiencing.

Others Read Your Energy:

I have a close friend named Sue. Whenever we talk, I can feel Sue in my invading my space checking me out. Sue has no boundaries. She does the same thing with all of her friends and ends up taking on all their problems. Her tendency to pick up others' problems can be very draining for Sue. Sue says she does this because it keeps her safe knowing what others are feeling. I taught her how to use the roses and connect to God Source energy and she can get the same knowingness of safety now without taking on other people's energy.

Cleaning Out Your Space:

Next, you may want to go inside your head and clean all the

people out. Get in a quiet place and take in a couple of deep breaths. Next, visualize you inside your head. Notice all the other people in your head with you. It is time for them to leave. You are the only one who is allowed in your head. Use your imagination on how you want to get them out of your head.

You can put them in a bubble out in front of you. Then, when the bubble is full of all the people, you can send it up to the sun and dissolve it. Or, you can suck all the people up into a huge vacuum cleaner. This modality is really a powerful way to keep your energy clean and pure.

The important part is to get all the people out of your head. You might have a few people that will resist and not want to leave. Keep working with these people until you can get them all out of your head. The resistant people are usually the ones in your life that do not want you to grow and heal. These people usually do not want to give up the control that they have over you either.

Cleaning your space (your head) helps you gain back your control and power over your own life. This does not mean that you do not love these people; it simply means that they do not belong in your head. Cleaning out your head will also help to quiet the noise in there so you can hear your own inner guidance.

After the people are all out of your head, then you want to decorate the inside of your head. Put a big chair in the center of your head so that you can look out your own eyes. You can put whatever colors you want in your head and add decorations. Make it feel peaceful to you. The purpose is to get rid of the people in your head that are running your show, telling you what to do. These are the little voices of mom saying, 'don't do that,' or the voice of your father, spouse, and siblings. Now it is just you and your inner guidance inside your head.

Challenges:
One client had a challenge with her mother. She would remove

her from her head and a few minutes later she would notice that her mom was back again. It took her a couple of weeks to be able to keep her mom completely out of her head.

In this instance, you would want to do the following: Pretend your mouth is open and your tongue is a bridge. Picture a clear bubble out in front of you and ask all the people in your head to leave, cross the bridge and go into the bubble. Clean out all of the negative thoughts and feelings sending them into the bubble as well.

Next, pull all the old self-destructive scripts from your past that do not serve you and put those in the bubble. You know the scripts I am talking about, the ones where your parents, siblings, friends, teachers, and others told you negative things about you and you believed them. This is any script that does not support you in your magnificence.

For example, Gayle's mom told her several times that she could not manage money and that tape played over and over in her head every time she thought about money. Since we get what we focus on, Gayle's mom was right. Gayle could not manage her money. After getting her mom and the tape out of her head, Gayle learned to manage her money.

Now, check the three-foot circle you are in and notice what energy, people, or thoughts are in your three-foot gold bubble. If you have people or negative emotions in your three-foot circle, put them in a clear bubble and send the bubble out to the sun blowing the bubble up in the sun. Keep doing this until your three-foot circle is clear.

Then, go inside your head and decorate your head. Put a chair in the middle of your head and sit in the chair looking out from behind your closed eyes. You can use any colors or decorations that feel good to you. No one is allowed in your head, just you.

Now, some of you may not want to blow the clear bubble up in the sun, so just dissolve the bubble into the sun. There is no right or wrong way, just find what works for you. These are tools to start with, but you can certainly change the color of the roses, or the color of the clear bubble etc. Do not get hung up on the details, just do the process the way that feels right to you. The purpose is to clear out the negative energy. You should be able to feel if the people and negative thoughts are out of your head.

As you work with these tools, you will discover what works best for you. If you are having a problem with this technique, I would then say that you have some resistance to healing yourself. If that is the case, you will want to roll the resistance up out of your body. Keep reading and you will come to that technique.

Meditation:
I believe meditation is essential to your well-being. I have been meditating for over twenty years. I have many clients that tell me they can't seem to quiet their minds enough to meditate. It takes practice. Start with just five minutes every morning. If you can't love yourself enough to give yourself five minutes, then I would encourage you to determine why you are not worthy of love.

Below is a detailed plan for meditating. Do not make it complicated. The important part is to just focus on your breath. I counted the breaths in my head when I started to help me stay focused. My mind was so cluttered back then that is was difficult for me to focus just like many of my clients. Clean all of the negative thoughts and people out of your head before you start your breathing. Then you are ready to focus on the breath. Start with just five minutes a day and every couple of weeks add another minute. Work up to a routine that last approximately15-20 minutes everyday.

You can even meditate ten minutes in the morning and ten minutes before you go to bed. Meditating before bed helps clear out some of the days problems so that you can sleep more peacefully. So many people have sleep disorders. But if they would learn to meditate and let all their stresses go, they would not have sleep problems.

Steps for Meditating:

Find a quiet place where you will not be interrupted. It is important to wear comfortable clothing. Sit cross-legged on a cushion or on the floor or in a chair. Get comfortable. Keep your back and head straight. You can close your eyes or leave them half opened and unfocused. Minimize your movement and relax.

Breathe from your belly, not your chest. Inhale through your nose and exhale through your mouth. Focus on your breathing, fixing your attention on the inhalation and exhalation. Notice how the air feels entering and exiting your body. You can count your breathing. In two, three, four, hold it two three, four, exhale two three, four, five, six, seven and eight. Keep doing this over and over staying focused on your breathing.

The purpose of meditation is to become fully aware of the present moment. As you breathe, watch your thoughts come and go. Do not fixate on any one idea or thought. Simply notice them and let them go. If you get distracted, just bring your focus back to your breathing.

Keep breathing and refocusing for as long as you want. Usually 15-20 minutes is a good time frame. Gradually open your eyes; then ground back into your body and slowly stand. You will feel refreshed.

Chakras:

Your chakras are energy ports located in your body (see Diagram A). Running energy in your body will assist you in opening your chakras and cleaning out the negative energy that is stored in them. (The technique of running energy is discussed later.)

When your chakras become clogged with negative emotions, your energy bogs down and illness occurs. Doreen Virtue describes your chakras the best when she said; "they are like a ceiling fan with overlapping fan blades rotating in a clockwise fashion."[1] The chakras have the ability to open and close.

Opening your chakras allows more energy to pass through them. The more closed they are, obviously, less energy goes through them.

Briefly, I will discuss the purpose of each chakra. If you want more details, you can find books that are completely devoted to the study of chakras.

Your *Root Chakra* is associated with the color red. (See Diagram A for the location of the chakras.) This is where survival instincts are stored. Fears, worries and concerns about money and safety are stored as dark spots in this chakra. If this chakra is wide open, it means that you are in a space of fear or survival. If it is mostly closed, then it means that you are not in that survival mode, but a more trusting place.

Your second chakra is called your *Sacral Chakra*. It is associated with the color orange. It is associated with sexuality, sensuousness, sensitivity, compassion and emotions. People that are very emotional and empathic tend to have this chakra wide open. This chakra is also associated with beliefs about appetites and desires. Of course, this can result in addictions. Because I am very sensitive to other people's energy, when I am doing readings for people, I close this chakra way down so that I do not pick up their emotions. Later in this chapter, I will explain how to shut your chakras down.

The third chakra is the *Solar Plexus*. It is associated with the color yellow. This chakra is your power center. It is also connected to independence, creativity and control. This is the place in which you assimilate and discern all information including the impact others have on you. Women typically have this chakra partially closed because they have a tendency to give their power away. Teenagers that are trying to be independent usually have this chakra wide open so that they can assert their power. People that try to control others have this chakra open.

The fourth chakra is the *Heart Chakra*. This chakra is associated with the color green like Jade. Your heart chakra is the energy center that is associated with beliefs pertaining to love and relationships. You receive and give love through your heart chakra. The more hurt and pain a person endures, the more their heart chakra closes. If you have any darkness in your heart chakra, it is probably connected to fears about being hurt. People that do not have a lot of joy in their lives have this chakra partially closed.

The fifth chakra is the *Throat Chakra*. It is connected to light blue. This particular energy center associated with speaking your truth and asking for your needs to be met. If you do not speak your truth or stand up for yourself, typically you will experience a lot of throat problems. In that case your chakra is more closed than someone that says what is on their mind.

The sixth chakra is dark blue. It occasionally flashes with white and purple sparkles of light. This is your *Third Eye Chakra*. It is in between your eyes and slightly higher. Your third eye is an oval shape eye sitting horizontally looking back at you allowing you to look within. This is the chakra where clairvoyance and visions come from. This chakra is used to understand the vastness of all things past, present, and future.

The seventh chakra represents your *Crown Chakra*. This energy center operates so that you can connect directly to God and your Higher Self. This chakra is a majestic purple color. Darkness in this area indicates fear in connecting to Divine Wisdom and Guidance, your angels, and God.

Managing Your Chakras:

Now that you have an understanding of your chakras and where they are located in your body, I want to explain how you can open and close them. Let's start at your root chakra. Pretend that you place a control gauge on in, much like a hand dial thermostat. The dial goes from zero to one hundred. Tune into your root chakra and see what the setting is. The closer to zero the more closed your chakra is and the closer to a hundred the more open your chakra is.

Just trust your knowingness and see how open or closed your root chakra is. The more open the more fear. This chakra is associated with money worries and survival. Now, I want you to turn your dial down to ten, closing the root chakra down almost completely. How does that feel? If you were really in a space of fear I would suggest turning this chakra down to ten and see if that shifts your fear somewhat.

Let's proceed to the second chakra and put a dial on it. Ask what level your dial is set to. Trusting your gut feeling, what is your dial set? Turn it down to ten. Someone who is very emotional and sensitive to other people's emotions would want to close this chakra down a little.

Your third chakra is your power center. Women should set their dial at seventy and men at fifty. Women have a tendency to give their power away. Therefore, it would be good to open that chakra up so that you are able to stand in your power. Men have a tendency to over power others, so for you, it would be good to close your chakra down to fifty.

Go ahead and put a gauge on your fourth chakra, which is your heart. How open is your heart? The goal would be to learn to open your heart fully. It may be uncomfortable to open it to one hundred to start, especially if it has been closed for a long time. There can be some fear and vulnerability associated with opening your heart.

Your fifth chakra is your throat. When Sue learned this process at one of the workshops I teach, her throat chakra gauge was set at about thirty. She realized that it was no wonder she had a lot of sore throats. It was very difficult for her to speak her truth to some people, especially family. The goal for this chakra would to open it up and speak from a place of love and compassion.

Your sixth chakra is your third eye. Most people have kept that fairly closed because they were either taught to do so or they had fears for what they saw as a child. What does your gauge say about your third eye? Again, the goal would be to open it to a place of comfort for you. Open your third eye as much as you can. Practice opening up your third eye more every day until you reach your comfort zone.

Your seventh chakra should be completely open. What does your gauge say? This is your connection to source or God. Keep working with this chakra until you can fully open it.

Finally, you have ear chakras. They are above your ears and slightly slanted. Put a gauge on these chakras and see whether they are opened and how much. Your ear chakras allow you to hear the spirit world. Opening your chakras will help you to hear your angels and any other higher guidance you are connected to.

In summary, you ideally want your first and second chakras turned down closing them to around ten to twenty. You want your third chakra at fifty for men and seventy for women. Then you want all the other chakras at one hundred fully open. Now they will not stay this way all the time. They are going to open and close based on what is going on with you and the people you are around.

Begin to notice them and learn how to adjust them. When I am doing readings or working with clients I turn my first and second chakras down to ten, my third at seventy and open the rest to one hundred. This way I am not picking up my client's fear or other emotions, I am not giving my power away and I am coming from a place of love and compassion. My third eye is open and my connection to God is strong. This makes for a good reading that is coming from a place higher than myself.

Running Energy:
Now that you understand your chakras, let's learn how to run energy in your body. Running energy will open your chakras and clean them out. This will bring up deeper emotions that you have stored in your body. Please review Diagrams B, C and D to gain a better understanding of how this energy is going to run

in your body.

Sitting comfortably go ahead and get grounded. Put your six roses in place and ground them. Visualize your big golden sun above your head. Next, bring the gold energy down filling up your body head to toe. Then spread the gold energy out into a three-foot circle filling it full of gold energy. Go all the way down into the earth about a foot below the ground and tuck the gold energy into your grounding cord.

On the bottom of your feet you have chakras. You also have two energy channels that run up the front of your legs all the way up your thighs. To run energy in your body you would start with picking a color you want to use. Use Diagram B to help you visualize the channels in your legs.

Visualize a color of earth energy from the ground. Now, bring this color of earth energy up through the chakras in the bottom of your feet. Keep bringing this earth energy up the channels in your legs all the way up your thighs. Bring the earth energy all the way up to your root chakra, twirl it around and then send it down through your grounding cord back to mother earth.

You can use any color you want. Change colors any time you want. Play with this and have fun seeing which color moves out the energy blocks in your legs. This will help you feel energetic and able to move forward.

Now, you are going to pull in some cosmic energy. You will reach up into the heavens and find a color that works for you. You can also change this color anytime you want. Bring this color of cosmic energy down into the top of your head (see Diagram C). Continue bringing the cosmic energy down and notice that it will split into two channels down the back of your head. One channel is on each side of the center of the back of your head. When it hits your shoulders it splits into four channels. Two channels run down each side of your spine all the way to the tailbone or root chakra area.

In the root chakra, you want to mix the cosmic energy with the earth energy. Next, you bring 100% cosmic energy and 15% earth energy up the front of your body (see Diagram D). There are two channels on each side of center where you will bring this energy all the way up to the throat. At the throat the energy splits. The two most center channels go straight up the neck, face and out the top of the head just like a whale spout. The two outer channels will split into two more channels each going down the inside of your arms and shooting out the palm of your hands.

Run your energy for a few moments and see how that feels. Notice how your chakras begin to turn more easily as this energy moves them. It is recommended that you do this entire process of grounding, putting out your roses, bringing down the sun, and running your energy every morning to start your day. Then quickly check your head and three-foot circle to see if anyone or anything is in your space that does not belong there. There should be nothing in your space but you. If there is anyone or any negative emotions in your three-foot circle, put them in a bubble and send them out to the sun and blow them up or dissolve them into the sun.

Once you start energy running in the morning, the energy will run all day. However, you will need to check your grounding cord, roses, and golden sun throughout the day. If your roses wilt or die, replace them with new ones. In fact, you can replace the grounding cord, roses, and sun throughout the day if you want. This procedure takes practice, but after you have done it a few times it becomes second nature.

Remember that the purpose of these exercises is to set your boundaries and put protection around you so that you are not picking up other people's negative energy.

Pulling Cords:

Have you ever heard the phrase, "just cut the cord" when someone is referring to letting a person go? Cutting the cord is actually a practice in many different spiritual teachings. In the

Hawaiian teachings of Huna, as discussed in *Fundamentals of Hawaiian Mysticism* by Charlotte Berney, [2] cords are referred to as AKA cords. They are silvery, white cords. Some of these cords are as thin as threads. I have seen some as big as three inches in diameter. Cords are connections to other people.

People unconsciously attach cords to other people to hang onto them or to control that person. The problem with having cords in your body is that they suck your energy and can cause physical pain.

The only cords you would want in your body are the ones connecting you to your children under the age of eighteen. All other cords should be pulled, even if you do not know whom the cord is connected to. I will explain how to stay connected to children over eighteen and spouses in a few minutes.

I see the cords, but you may not have clairvoyant sight yet, so you would want to feel for them. Take your hand and start at the top of your head. Slowly run it down and around the front part of your body. Does the energy all feel the same or do you notice any hot or cold spots? The hot or cold spots are usually cords that block the energy in your body. If you can reach your entire backside, then check that as well. If not, have someone check the backside of your body for you. Or you could just trust your knowingness and check your back yourself.

Should you find any cords, you would want to pull them out. You pull these cords out like you are pulling a weed making sure you get the root. Just pretend you are grabbing a weed and start pulling on it until you sense that you have pulled the cord and root completely out of your body. This could take a minute or so especially if the root is really deep. Now you want to fill that space up so that you do not have an empty pocket. Bring the color gold in until that empty space is full of gold energy. If you just cut the cord off leaving the root, it can still cause illness. Therefore, you want to pull the cord and root.

You may or may not be able to sense who corded you. You do

not need to know that answer to pull the cord. You want to recognize that on some level you allowed this person to cord you. People cord each other to stay connected, to have control over them, or because they just want to suck their energy, thus the energy vampire phrase.

I can usually tell when my mom cords me. She seems to cord me in my right ovary. So, when my ovary starts to ache for no reason, I check to see if there are any cords and sure enough, there is one. I pull the cord out. Then I bring gold energy into my ovary and the pain will go away immediately. My mom can tell when I have pulled the cord. She will call and tell me she does not feel like we are connected any more.

What I decided to do with my mom was to connect a cord with her so that she would not cord my body. I pictured a cord from my heart going out about ten feet and a cord from her heart out about ten feet. I connected those cords in a gold ring. That way Mom feels connected; but she is not draining my energy or causing me physical pain.

You will want a connection to your spouse and children over eighteen. I discuss kids under eighteen in a few minutes. You visualize a cord coming out of your heart and one coming out of your spouse or partner's heart. Bring both the cords out to a neutral space between you. Make the space at least six feet out from your heart and six feet out from their heart. Connect those cords in a gold ring for partners.

Do the same thing for your children over eighteen, but connect them with a rainbow or gold ring. I use both rainbow and gold rings; you use whatever feels right to you. This allows you to be connected without draining energy or trying to control each other. Children under the age of eighteen should have a cord from their heart to your heart directly. You would want a strong connection to your younger children because you are still raising them. Check to be sure that the cord is from heart to heart. I see many parents that cord in the child's belly to gain control over them. However, it usually leads to power struggles. Pull the cord out of the belly and replace it in the heart. Your relationship will be more loving and less controlling on both parts.

I have a couple of granddaughters that I am very connected to; therefore, I have cords attached with rainbow rings out about six feet from my body to each of the girls individually.

I have other family members and friends, but I do not have cords attached to them. We automatically connect when I see them or talk to them, but they do not need cords sucking my energy or me taking energy from them.

Opening Your Heart:

Many people have closed hearts. For example, one client, Trisha had put a box around her heart. Around the box she put chains. She had to find a pretend key to unlock the big padlock on the chains to take them off. Then Trisha was able to remove the box that kept her heart closed.

Another client had some sort of armor, like the knights wore in the old days, wrapped around her heart. She had to create a laser beam to open the seams in the armor so she could peal the armor off freeing her heart.

Whatever is blocking your heart needs to come off, so be open to seeing if you have some sort of protection around your heart. The protection keeps love from coming in and going out. It's time to open your heart.

Forgiveness Method:

This procedure is very important. You need to forgive everyone in your life that does not support your magnificence. This would be anyone that you are holding negative thoughts toward or people that have wronged you.

I want you to pretend that there is a stage out in front of you. You are floating in front of the stage and about a foot higher than the stage. Now, bring up the first person you want to forgive and put him/her on the stage. I want you to pretend that you have opened up the top of your head. Bring white light down through the top of your head filling up your whole body. Pretend you can visualize an AKA cord connecting you together from heart to heart. Flow the white light from your body through the cord into their heart filling up their entire body with white light. Now you are both filled with white light.

Next, say everything you need to say to that person. Then, hear what you need to hear them say to you. Then, tell them you forgive them, forgive yourself, give them permission to forgive you and permission to forgive themselves. Now, pull the cord out of your heart, root and all, and send them off out into the light releasing them to their wholeness. The light is behind the sun. The light is the great central sun that feeds light into the sun. Or, if you just visualize them going up to the sun that is good.

Bring the next person up on the stage and do the exact same process. It might be best to start with a clone of yourself and forgive yourself for any wrong you have caused yourself. Then bring your mom and dad up on the stage one at a time and do the same process with them. Next, bring up anyone else that needs forgiveness or that you need to forgive.

When you have completed everyone you can think of, just ask if there are any other people that need your forgiveness and complete the process with him/her. Then you would want to bring up any negative thought forms, fears or beliefs that are holding you back and do the process with these negative forms.

Forgiveness is a very important aspect to healing. Use this technique whenever you feel the need to forgive someone and get forgiveness from someone. When done with this process, bring gold energy down and fill up your body. It is important to always fill back up with gold energy whenever you have released negative energy. If you do not fill back up, you will fill empty inside.

Tad James in his book *Lost Secrets of Ancient Hawaiian Huna*,[3] discusses many Huna practices that are were used by the Hawaiians in ancient times. The process of forgiveness that you just learned is knows as Ho'oponopono.

Bubble Technique:

This is the fun part because you are releasing unwanted negative energy and gaining back your power. After you have grounded, set your roses, put your golden sun around you and cleared your head, you are now ready to start releasing your "stuff."

Picture a clear bubble out in front of you and pull all the fear you have out of your body with your hand and put it in it. Go back to the core event. The core event could be past lives, or it could be fear passed down genealogically from mom's family or dad's side of the family (or both). Or the core event could be somewhere between conception to age ten. Just trust yourself to float all the way back the root cause the first event of fear. Pull all that fear out of your body and into the bubble. It can be fear in general or specific fear. Let's start with any fear you have about healing, then add the fear you might have about releasing all your 'stuff' into the bubble. Add all the fear of the unknown and any fear of what others' are going to think of you when you heal. Pull it out of your body and put it into the bubble.

Keep adding to the bubble any other fear that comes up for you. Now put your resistance to healing in the bubble. Add your family and friends' resistance to your growing and healing into the bubble. Pull it all out of your body into the bubble. When the bubble is nice and full, send it all the way out to the center of the universe and blow the bubble up. As the bubble is blowing up, picture your positive power coming back to you in streams of gold energy into a big golden sun above your head.

When the sun is nice and full, reach up and bring it down. Fill up your body head to toe. Spread the gold energy out into the three-

foot circle of roses and all the way down to the ground. A foot below the earth; tuck the gold energy into your grounding cord.

Now, the key here is not to get hung up on right or wrong ways of doing this. Just go with it and allow it to flow. For whatever reason, if gold does not work for you, then use another color. Gold is one of the highest vibrational colors and should work. It is more important to release the negative emotions out of your body and out of your space than to get hung up in the process of doing it perfectly.

Now that you have this part down, continue releasing whatever negative emotions come up for you. You might want to make a list of negative emotions and then sit down in the morning and again in the evening and clear everything on your list.

You can just pull the negative energy out of your body or you can use the Time Line Therapy detailed earlier in the book. Using Time Line Therapy helps you to go to the root cause so that the entire pattern can be healed. Just pulling the negative emotions out of your body is pulling only the emotion that you are currently feeling and not clearing out the entire pattern. Sometimes you only have time to do the feeling you are experiencing at the moment. The goal would to later take the time to clear all the feelings attached to the pattern.

It is important to go back to the core event, the root cause of that emotion and put it in the bubble. If you do not go to the core, you are just pulling out layers. That means that you will not get the entire pattern. Just allow yourself to float all the way back into your past. Take a deep breathe and float all the way back to the first event, the event that when you release it, will allow all those emotions to disappear as an issue in your life.

I know you don't know what that first event is, but if you were to know, was it in past lives, in the womb or from conception to age ten? Just trust your intuition that whatever comes up is the correct answer. Just float back to that time and put all those negative feelings, along with any people from that event, into a bubble out in front of you. Then as you slowly come forward to the present, you want to add all other events or emotions that are connected to that first event. Put them all in a bubble. Keep filling that bubble full of all those negative emotions.

Now, send the bubble out to the sun and blow it up and picture your power coming back to you in streams of gold into a golden sun above your head. When the sun is full, bring the golden sun down and fill up your body head to toe. Spread the gold energy all the way out to your three-foot circle of roses and down into the ground tucking it into your grounding cord.

Mary's Experience:

For example, Mary was clearing disappointment at not getting what she wanted. The disappointment came up because she was disappointed that she did not receive some money. She floated all the way back to the root cause, the first event of disappointment. She immediately felt that the disappointment originated in past lives. She put the disappointment and all the other emotions attached to the event into a bubble that I had her visualized out in front of her. Then, she started floating towards her present. She noticed that in the womb she also felt disappointment. She could see that her mom and dad had wanted a boy; instead they got a girl. She put those emotions in the bubble.

She continued coming towards the present and saw lots of little events centering on disappointment. She put all of these incidents into the bubble. Now, her bubble was really full. She continued coming towards the present adding all the other events and feelings of disappointment. In fact, the last disappointment had initiated the entire process.

When the process felt complete, she sent the bubble out to the center of the universe. Then, she visualized the bubble blowing up into the sun. Finally, as the bubble is blowing up, she pictured her positive power coming back to her in streams of gold into a big golden sun above her head.

Now, the sun above her head felt full of golden energy. She mentally reached up and punctured the sun bringing the gold energy down into the top of her head. Here, I had her continue bringing the golden energy down filling up her body head to toe. Next, she spread the sun all the way out to her roses. Finally, she spread the golden energy all the way down into the ground and tucked the golden energy into her grounding cord about a foot below the ground. She felt much better.

When you remove negative feelings, I would suggest that you replace that space or energy with positive energy. Picture your gold sun filled with self-confidence, love, knowingness, or whatever it is you want. Then just bring those gold suns down filling up your body with those positive emotions.

This particular process will help clear out a lot of your old emotions. However, if you feel like you are carrying the emotions in your body, then you would want to use the Roll-Up Method.

Roll-up Technique:

Here is another interesting technique that is great for letting go of the people you carry. You want to use this technique when you feel you are carrying your kids or anyone else and their problems inside your body.

Here is an example of what occurred with Terry, one of my clients. Terry, felt really bogged down and was carrying a lot of worry that I could see was not hers. She was carrying her two kids' and their problems inside her body. Even though her kids are grown, as a mother she often listened to their problems and then took them on as her own.

Her oldest son, Jon, was going through a really difficult child custody battle. Terry was carrying Jon's burden inside her body.

Terry knew it was draining her energy, but she just could not seem to release this tendency of hers to carry her children.

In fact, the more anger and fear Jon felt, the angrier Terry became. At the time, Terry could not see the anger and fear. She was blinded by her son's desperation to have his daughter under his wing. Emotions ran high and low for four years; they were in and out of courts fighting for what seemed like a never-ending battle.

One day, Terry realized what this stressful experience was doing to her. Accordingly, she pulled away. She needed to stop carrying the burden. By holding onto the emotions, Terry was keeping the case from being resolved in a positive manner. She was only adding fuel to the fire. Terry began to re-evaluate the situation.

This was her son's battle; it didn't need to be hers. She needed to hold the intent that whatever served the highest good of all would be the resolution. Terry could not seem to let the anger go. She was able to mentally let the anger go, but she could still feel anger in her body. I taught her how to use the following technique to pull her son and all the emotions out of her body. This resulted in releasing the entire situation to a Higher Power.

In order to affect the release, I had her bend down to her feet and tune into all the feelings surrounding her son, Jon and Cathy, the mother of her granddaughter. She could feel the anger, rage, hurt, disappointment, sadness, guilt and pain. She began to roll Jon and Cathy and these emotions up her legs. I had her visualize going inside her body and rolling all the emotions and people up her body. I had her just stay in tune with the emotions and rolled all of them up her legs, hips, stomach, chest, heart, throat, face, and head and then pulled Jon, Cathy and the emotions all out of the top of her head. I had her call Jon and Cathy along and roll them up her body. Next, I had her pull and pull until she could feel that Jon and Cathy and all the negative emotions surrounding their issues were finally expelled from her body out the top of her head. She dumped all the negative energy out in front of her on the floor.

Now pretend your fingers are scissors and cut the energy off at the top of your head. Put all that negative energy out in front of you. Next, visualize Jon and Cathy in front of you as well. Here, you gather up the negative emotions and handed them to Jon and Cathy. The negative emotions were really Jon and Cathy's, not Terry's. As Terry handed the negative emotions back to them, I had her say:

"I am giving these emotions and energy back to you, not to hurt you or cause you harm, but because I no longer choose to carry you or your burdens. I choose to be whole and complete. I thank you for the lessons I have learned in carrying these emotions. I forgive you and forgive myself. I give you permission to forgive me and forgive yourself. I release all these emotions. I release you to your wholeness."

At this point, I had Terry visualized Archangel Michael come and take Jon, Cathy, and all of the negative emotions out to the center of the universe to be re-charged and brought back as healthy energy. Then, she filled a golden sun up with feelings of peace and brought the gold energy down through the top of her head and all the way down into her body. As she began filling up her entire body from head to toe with this gold energy, she immediately noticed how much lighter and more peaceful she felt.

It is important to remember that when you release negative emotions from your body, you always want fill back up with gold or white light. If you do not, you are leaving empty energy space and you will feel empty.

Cutting Energy Out of Your Body:

Sometimes you can feel fear (or whatever emotion) stuck right in your belly. Rolling it up is not necessary if it is just stuck in your belly. Therefore, this method goes straight to the heart of that stuck energy.

Close your eyes and take in a couple of deep breaths. Relax. Now, focus on the blocked energy (whether belly, chest, heart, or where ever). In your mind's eye literally take your hand and pull that blocked energy out of your belly. Keep pulling and pulling that blocked energy out of your body.

Now, with your other hand take the first two fingers and pretend they are a point of a laser beam. Visualize you going inside your body. With your laser beam energy, burn the negative energy out of your body as you are pulling it out. Keep doing this until you get all the negative energy out of your body.

When you are done, you will feel empty inside. Then you bring in gold energy to fill back up.

Shrink Your Ego:

Close your eyes. Take a couple of deep breaths and relax. Take your hand and put in on the back of your head. Grab your ego from inside the back of your head. Bring your ego around in front. With your ego in your hand, look at it with your third eye, or your knowingness or your feelings.

What does your ego look like? Is it male or female? Is it positive or negative? Does it hold a lot of fear?

Thank your ego for all it has done for you. Now shrink your ego down to the size of a pinhead. Place your ego back behind your ear. Tell it to stay there until you ask it to come out.

I would suggest doing this process everyday until you gain control over your ego. If you have a strong ego, you may have to do it several times a day. Now, visualize going down inside your heart and living in that space instead of your ego. You will notice how your choices will be completely different coming from your heart versus your ego.

Your ego is still there and available anytime you feel you need to use it. Just go back up into your head and I assure you, your ego will pop back out.

Changing Patterns or Beliefs:

The best way to change a belief is to go to a NLP practitioner. He or she can help you discover why you persist in hanging on to the beliefs you have. The NLP Practitioner can suggest ways to help in the reprogramming process. (NLP Practitioners are found on the Internet; search under Neuro-Linguestic Programming.)

The following is a general overview of how to change a belief.

Think of a belief about yourself that you would like to be different. This should be a belief that limits you in some way. I want you to think of that belief that you would rather not have. Put that belief aside for a moment.

Now, I want you to think of something you are doubtful about. It might be true, or it might not be. Next, I want you to notice how those two experiences of belief and doubt are different. Is your belief a big picture or small? It is bright, vivid and detailed. Or is it small, dim and fuzzier? Does it fill up the entire frame or is there little room for the background.

This is much like adjusting your T.V. set. What is the picture like? Notice the differences. Now, take the list of differences and test them one at a time in order to find out which ones are the most powerful in changing your belief.

For example, take your picture of belief and try making it smaller. Does that change it to doubt? If not, take the bright and vividness and change it to dim and drab. Does that change your belief to doubt?

If not, take the detailed picture and make it blurry. Then, go to a stable picture and make it flashing. Next, try a framed picture and go to no frame. Then, try little background to lots of background. Is the picture right in front of you or off to the side?

One of these modalities is going to change your belief to one of doubt.

First, start thinking about your belief now and be sure you think about it in positive terms. Think of what you want to believe, not what you don't want to believe.

Second, I want you to frame that belief in terms of a process or ability that would result in you getting that goal.

Third, I want you to take some time to imagine how you would act differently if you already had this new belief. Think of any ways in which this change could be a problem for you, or the people who are close to you. If you can't think of any way that it could be a problem, than that is your new belief. Set this new belief aside for a moment.

Fourth, I want you to take that big picture of the belief you do not like and move it all the way over to where your doubt is. As you do that, the picture will lose its frame and get dimmer, small, and blurry and start flashing. When that picture flashes off, have the picture of the old belief disappear, and then have the picture of the new belief flash back on.

Fifth, take the picture of your new belief and move it back to the center of your visual field. As you do this, notice how it develops a frame and gets bigger, brighter, sharper and more vivid.

Richard Bandler goes into detail on how to change your beliefs in his book, *Using Your Brain for a Change*.[4]

You have learned many different techniques throughout this book. These techniques only work if you use them. If you suspect that you have major trauma in your past, you would serve yourself to seek help in healing those wounds. There are many wonderful qualified people that have the ability to assist you in healing your past. It is easier to work with someone that can guide you and assist you in bringing to your awareness the events and emotions that need healing.

If you are ready to start healing and growing or have already started, you will find these techniques very helpful. Healing is not a one day, one time process. Healing is on-going.

It is important to look at each event in your life as a lesson. Then, ask each lesson what it is trying to teach you. As you begin paying attention to your life, you will realize that your life is speaking to you. Your body is speaking to you. It is time to listen. You will gain so much awareness of who you really are and what you are here learning when you pay attention to what is in your life.

I also believe it is important to be grateful for all that you have. I spend time every night either writing down what I am grateful for or just speaking about it in my prayers. It is important because it raises your vibrational frequency to a higher level by focusing on the good. You are sending out that high vibration to the universe and then more of the same high vibration comes back to you.

So many people focus on what they don't want. It is time to focus on what you do want. This is the time to heal from your past, discard all the old that no longer serves you, and then focus on where you want to go with your life. Focus on finding joy, love, and happiness.

Chapter 9

Conclusion

"By three methods we may learn wisdom: first, by reflection,
which is noblest; second, by imitation, which is easiest; and
third by experience, which is the bitterest."

Confucius

What You Learned:

You have just learned how to change your life from victim to empowerment. You have learned many different patterns, behaviors and beliefs that might be keeping you from obtaining your goals. Later, you were given the tools to move through your challenges. The final step is up to you. That step is doing the work to change your life. I know you are up for your journey or you would not have been drawn to read this book. Enjoy the process! Life is supposed to be pleasurable, not so heavy and not all work. Life is not supposed to be suffering, but meant to be joyful.

It is much easier if you take the time to clear out these issues when it is convenient for you, versus putting it off and letting the universe pick the time. As you grow, you gain more power over your space and you become peaceful inside. Your life starts to flow in incredibly wonderful ways. Love you have always been looking for shows up. Money you have always wanted suddenly appears.

You begin to gain more access to your spiritual gifts and receive more of your guidance from God, Angels, and Spirit Guides. Life is good. While at times your journey may seem endless, recognize how far you have actually come.

The Angels taught me a new technique about a year ago that I call Cellular Healing. I am able to pull out patterns and beliefs at the cellular level from past lives, in the womb and from birth to current age. I am very grateful for all the teachings. The more I clear my past, the more spiritual gifts I am given.

I am now able to manifest at a very fast pace. For example, the day before Thanksgiving I needed my family room carpet shampooed and did not have time to do it myself. I simply asked the universe to take care of it.

About three hours later, my doorbell rang. There was a lady at the door. "Hi, we are testing a new rug shampoo in your neighborhood. We are offering to shampoo one room for free. Would you be interested?"

Of course I said yes. I thanked the universe for answering my request.

On another occasion, I had signed up for Direct TV, one of our cable companies. Then, a month later I purchased a DVD player for the T.V. in my bedroom. I am not mechanically inclined. I had absolutely no clue on how to hook up the DVD player up to the Direct TV. I asked my son and he did not know how to hook it up either.

I called Direct T.V. and they wanted to charge me $65 for the house call. I did not want to go that route. I realized I could probably stop a Direct T.V. truck and ask him if he would come and hook it up for me and I would pay him on the side. However, that would require me to leave the house, drive around to find a Direct T.V. truck.

Instead, I asked the universe, "Universe, I want Direct T.V. to come and hook up my DVD player. Thank you."

The next morning, my massage lady had just started my massage when my doorbell rang. She offered to answer the door since I was on the table. She came back and said, "Direct TV is here and wants to know if you need anything?"

I just laughed, thanked the universe and told her to show him in. I could go on with story after story, but you have the idea.

When you clear up your past, align yourself in trust with God (or the universe) and then focus on what you want, it happens.

Personal Fun Stories:

The Ring:

Several years ago when I lived in Plano, Texas I decided it might be fun to go to a Government Auction. My middle child, S.J. and his girlfriend said they would go with me to El Paso, Texas. My intention was to buy a vehicle at a really good price and then sell it in Plano and make some extra cash.

While looking over the items to be auctioned off, S.J. and I agreed on a truck that I would bid on. The bidding rolled around to some jewelry, specifically a matching ring and necklace. Before I knew what was happening, my bidding paddle was in the air and I was bidding on this matching ring and necklace.

I won the bid and my son just sat shaking his head.

S.J.: "Why did you bid on that necklace and ring? What do you need it for?"

Me: "I have no idea. It was almost as if I had no control over my arm. My paddle just seemed to pop up into the air."

S.J.: "That's just crazy, mom. Are you going to sell it?"

Me: "No, for some strange reason, I feel like it is mine. I will keep it."

I drove my car home while my son and his girlfriend followed in the newly purchased truck. I immediately put the ring on and I kept looking at it while I was driving. I just kept feeling it was mine.

I had been home a couple of weeks when I was meditating and for some reason I was twirling the ring. All of a sudden I had flashes of a past life.

I could see that I was in love with this man and that we were married. We lived in South America somewhere. For an anniversary

172

present he had this necklace and ring made special for me. They are both hand painted pieces of art with little flowers and leaves on them. Both the necklace and ring are very pretty pieces.

I could see how special I felt this jewelry was. The ring seemed more important to me than the necklace; perhaps because I wore the ring all the time and only wore the necklace on special occasions.

It was very clear that this was my ring from a past life. I could understand now while I had to have it. I also had the feeling that I could find the man from that lifetime that was my husband. I felt like he lived in Plano or close by.

A week later, I went to a metaphysical fair that was held every few months. I enjoyed going to be with like-minded people. I would get readings from a couple of the different psychics. One of them was a woman that did crystal ball gazing.

She took a hold of my hand and closed her eyes to start the reading. She had only been holding my hand a couple of seconds when she let it go and jumped back saying, "Wow, your ring just burnt my finger. What's going on with that ring?"

"I don't know. What do you see?" I replied.

She answered, "Your ring is a ring you had in a past life. You just recently reclaimed it. You were very much in love with the man that gave it to you. You will find him again in this lifetime, very soon."

Later in the week, while meditating again, I heard the angels tell me that the man that gave me the ring was a chiropractor. The angels said his first name was Glenn. They told me to go through the phone book and they would show me which chiropractor he was.

I opened the phone book and my eyes immediately focused on a chiropractor named Glenn.... I decided to call and schedule an appointment.

Upon arriving at his office, I realized how nervous I was. I was in an examine room trying to figure out what I would say to him. When he walked in, I noticed that he was tall and good-looking.

While he was giving my back an adjustment, I tried to work up the nerve to talk to him about the ring. I just could not think of what to say, so I said nothing. I went home disappointed in myself that I did not speak up. I was afraid he would think I was crazy.

I decided to pray about it and ask God to intervene and let me know what I should do. I really wanted to see if Glenn got any hits off the ring. I wanted to know if Glenn would have any sense of having known me before. I wanted confirmation.

I was still new to psychic phenomenon. I wanted confirmation about the information I was getting. I asked God, "God, please help me get the confirmation that I am looking for. Help me to be able to talk to Glenn and find the proof that I am after!"

I felt guided to go back to the chiropractic office for a second adjustment on my back. When I arrived, I discovered my appointment was with his partner. I wondered how seeing Dr. Scott was going to help me talk to Glenn. As I was pondering that question, Dr. Scott came in the examine room. We hit it off right away. I found Dr. Scott much easier for me to talk to, probably because I did not have an emotional attachment. We chatted easily about my work as a hypnotherapist. He was very interested and asked a lot of questions.

I told him why I was really in the office. I told him that I believed Glenn and I knew each other from a past life. I mentioned that I was hoping to get some proof. Dr. Scott thought it would be great if I hypnotized Glenn to see if Glenn would get any information on a past life of us together. I thought that was a great idea and he agreed to talk to Glenn about it.

Later that night, Glenn called me. He said, "Dr. Scott was telling me that you wanted to do a past life regression on me to see if we know each other from another life time."

"Yes, I would love to, if you are open to it. I do not want to give you any information because I do not want to front load your mind with any thoughts about us. I am working on a project and would love some verification one way or another. Would you be interested? No strings attached and no charge."

He agreed and we scheduled an appointment.

Past Life Regression:

Glenn was an easy subject to put in a hypnotic trance. I easily guided him into a past life that was connected to me. Glenn actually went to another lifetime that we had together where he was a doctor and I was his nurse.

I asked Glenn different questions about that lifetime. I moved him to another lifetime where we knew each other. This time he found the life I was searching for. Glenn confirmed that we lived in a city in South America. We were married and very much in love.

Glenn continued with more details about his job, our family, etc. I was excited to get the confirmation that he indeed had the ring and necklace specially made for me for an anniversary present.

This was all new information for Glenn. He needed some time to let it soak in. He called me a couple of weeks later and asked me to dinner. At dinner, Glenn told me that he had gone to a psychic to see if the information he saw during the past life regression was accurate. She confirmed that it was accurate.

Glenn and I were not really sure what to do with the information. We agreed that we would just be friends. Glenn was seeing a woman that he had feelings for. I was single, but not looking for a relationship. I had committed to raising my kids as a single mom, feeling that was less complicated for the kids and me. I was just happy to have confirmed that the information I was getting from my angels was correct.

APPENDIX

Quick Reference Chart
For Grounding, Roses, and Golden Sun

Step 1: Grounding – picture an old oak tree trunk from your tail bone going all the way down to the center of the earth. Root it into the earth until you can feel it tug you back into your body so that you are looking out through your own eyes. Spread your grounding cord out as wide as your hips.

Step 2: Put today's date on the grounding cord so you are grounded in present time. Then add a release button to the cord and release all the negative energy and anxious energy in your body down into the earth through the grounding cord.

Step 3: Put a four-foot tall rose out in front of you three-feet away. Put another rose behind you out three-feet and one on each side of you out three-fee. Add a rose above your head and one below your feet. Ground all six roses all the way down into mother earth and root them at the center of the earth. The roses can be any color you want.

Step 4: Picture a big golden sun above your head with a magnet in it. The magnet brings back all your energy that you have left at home, work, school, in your car or wherever. Fill the golden sun up with any other positive feelings such as havingness (I know that is not a real word). When it is nice and full, reach up in your mind's eye, puncture the sun and bring it down filling up your body head to toe. Now spread the golden sun out to your three-foot circle of roses. Bring the golden sun all the way down to the ground and about a foot below the ground tuck the golden sun into your grounding cord.

Step 5: Clean out your head. Get all of the people out because you are the only one that should be in your head. Put the people, negative thoughts and beliefs into a clear bubble out in front of you. Send the full bubble out to the sun and blow it up or dissolve it into the sun. Clean and decorate your head with you sitting in the center of it looking out your own closed eyes.

Step 6: Check your three-foot circle of roses and make sure that there are no people or negative thoughts inside your circle. If there are, put them into a bubble and send it out to the sun. Your three-foot circle should be completely clear. Your energy should be the only energy in your three-foot circle.

Step 7: Run energy using earth energy up the feet and up the channels in the front of your legs moving all the way up your thighs and in the root chakra. Swirl the earth energy around the root chakra cleaning it out. Bring cosmic energy down before above into the top of your head, then down into the channels in the back of your head, moving it down into the channels down your spine and mix it with the earth energy in the root chakra. Then bring 100% of cosmic energy up your front and 15% of earth energy. Bring the energy up your belly through the channels in the front all the way up to the throat where it splits and the two middle channels go straight up your face and out the top of the head. The other two channels split at the shoulder and go down the two channels on the inside of each arm until it shoots out your palms.

Diagram A – Chakras

Diagram B – Grounding Cord

Diagram C – Running Energy - Front

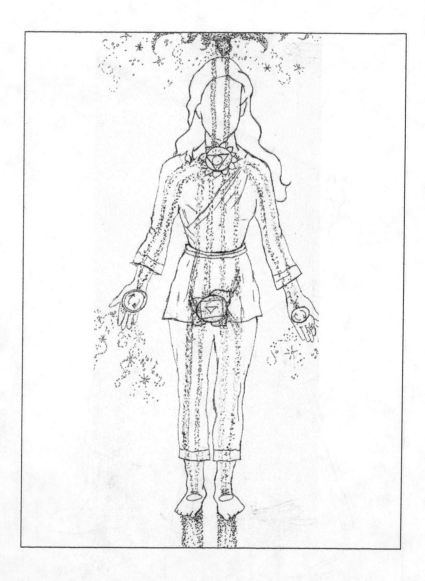

Diagram D – Running Energy – Back

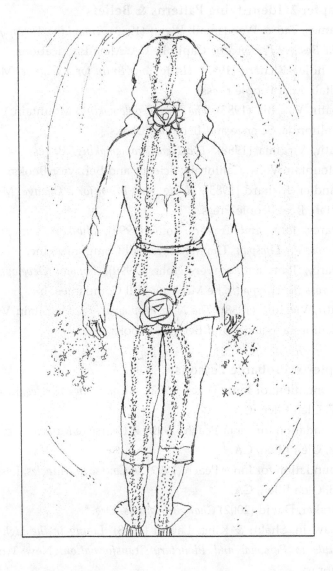

NOTES

Chapter 2: Identifying Patterns & Beliefs

1. James, Tad & Woodsmall, Wyatt (1988). *Time Line Therapy and the Basis of Personality*. Capitola, CA: Meta Publications.
2. Bandler, Richard (1985). *Using Your Brain for a Change*. Moab, Utah: Real People Press.
3. Satir, Virginia (1988). *The New Peoplemaking*. Mountain View, California: Science and Behavior Books.
4. Satir, Virginia (1988). *The New Peoplemaking*. Pages 134–135, Mountain View, California: Science and Behavior Books.
5. Bandler, Richard (1985). *Using Your Brain for a Change*. Moab, Utah: Real People Press.
6. Darcy, John and Travers, John (1999). *Human Development Across the Lifespan*. The McGraw-Hill Companies, Inc.
7. Darcy, John and Travers, John (1999). *Human Development Across the Lifespan*. The McGraw-Hill Companies, Inc.
8. Satir, Virginia (1988). *The New Peoplemaking*. Mountain View, California: Science and Behavior Books.

Chapter 3: Probable Lessons

1. Foundation for Inner Peace (1992). *A Course in Miracles*. Lesson 67, Glen Ellen, CA.
2. Foundation for Inner Peach (1992). *A Course in Miracles*, Lesson 68, Glen Ellen, CA.
3. Foundation for Inner Peach (1992). *A Course in Miracles*, Lesson 68, Glen Ellen, CA.
4. Straker, David (2002) *Changing Minds. Org*.
5. Gawain, Shakti & King, Laurel (1998). *Living in the Light: A guide to Personal and Planetary Transformation*. New World Library.
6. Gawain, Shakti & King, Laurel (1998). *Living in the Light: A guide to Personal and Planetary Transformation*. New World Library.

Chapter 4: Taking Responsibility
1. Ford, Debbie (1998). *The Dark Side of The Light Chasers.* New York, Berkley Publishing Group, Riverhead Books.
2. McKenna, Paul (2009). *I Can Make You Thin.* New York: Sterling Publishing.
3. Virtue, Doreen (1995). *Constant Craving: What your food cravings mean and how to overcome them.* Carlsbad, CA: Hay House, Inc.

Chapter 5: Inner Guidance
1. Foundation for Inner Peace (1992). *A Course in Miracles,* Lesson 223. Glen Ellen, CA.
2. Foundation for Inner Peace (1992). *A Course in Miracles,* Lesson 221. Glen Ellen, CA.
3. Brinkley, Dannion (1995). *Saved by the Light.* Harper Torch Publishing.

Chapter 6: Discover and Utilize Your Intuition
1. Virtue, Doreen (1999). *Divine Guidance: How to Have a Dialogue with God and Your Guardian Angels,* Carlsbad, CA: Hay House, Inc.
2. Intuitive Connections.net. /2003/ Vanauhen1.htm
3. Woodward, Mary Ann (1971). *Edgar Cayce's Story of Karma,* New: Coward-McCann.
4. Kautz, William, www.intuition.org/txt/kautz/htm
5. Hannah, Barbara (1976). *Jung, His Life and Work: A Biographical Memoir. New York:* G.P. Puttman & Sons.
6. Jung, Carl G. (1923) *Psychology Types,* Kindle Books.

Chapter 8: Techniques for Making Changes
1. Virtue, Doreen (1999). *Chakra Clearing Tape,* Carlsbad, CA: Hay House, Inc.
1. Berney, Charlotte (2000). *Fundamentals of Hawaiian Mysticism.* Freedom, CA: The Crossing Press.

4. James, Tad (1997). *Lost Secrets of Ancient Hawaiian Huna.* Honolulu, HI: Ka Ha O Hawai'i Foundation.
5. Bandler, Richard (1985). *Using Your Brain for a Change.* Moab, Utah: Real People Press.

BOOKS

O is a symbol of the world, of oneness and unity. In different cultures it also means the "eye," symbolizing knowledge and insight. We aim to publish books that are accessible, constructive and that challenge accepted opinion, both that of academia and the "moral majority."

Our books are available in all good English language bookstores worldwide. If you don't see the book on the shelves ask the bookstore to order it for you, quoting the ISBN number and title. Alternatively you can order online (all major online retail sites carry our titles) or contact the distributor in the relevant country, listed on the copyright page.

See our website www.o-books.net for a full list of over 500 titles, growing by 100 a year.

And tune in to myspiritradio.com for our book review radio show, hosted by June-Elleni Laine, where you can listen to the authors discussing their books.